LIP-READING
Principles and Practise

LIP-READING
Principles and Practise

BY

EDWARD B. NITCHIE, B.A.

FOUNDER OF THE NEW YORK SCHOOL FOR THE HARD-OF-HEARING,
(INCORPORATED), NOW THE NITCHIE SCHOOL OF LIP-READING,
INCORPORATED, AND ITS PRINCIPAL UNTIL 1917.

REVISED
BY
ELIZABETH HELM NITCHIE
AND
GERTRUDE TORREY

FREDERICK A. STOKES COMPANY
PHILADELPHIA   NEW YORK

Copyright, 1912, 1919, 1930, By Frederick A. Stokes Company

All rights reserved. No part of this work may be reproduced without the written permission of the publishers.

Printed in the United States of America

Edward B. Nitchie dedicated this book
"TO MY TEACHERS"

In behalf of all who have carried on his work
I dedicate its revision
TO HIM

MUSIC

The ruder strains of music are denied,
The music of the human voice is lost,
The gulf of silence ever grows more wide,
My bark sails noiseless o'er life's swelling tide.
    By soundless billows tost.

But waves of harmony forever roll,
Orchestral cadences e'er fall and rise:
The mysteries of the part within God's whole,
The eternal whisperings of the Over-Soul
    Still 'trance me to the skies.

Ceaseless I hear the God of Nature call
Where green and gold chant anthems in the wood;
The meadows, daisy-capped, the silver ball
Of evening, stars and surging ocean—all.
    All sing of Love and Good.

It is the symphony of symphonies
Within my soul I hear,—to live, to work,
To turn my back on stumbling yesterdays,
Soul-sure defeats may e'en be victories
    If e'er I fight, nor shirk.

INTRODUCTION

"LIP-READING Principles and Practise" was written by Edward B. Nitchie, founder of the New York School for the Hard of Hearing, now the Nitchie School of Lip-Reading, Inc. The development and perfecting of this meritorious work on lip-reading was an undertaking of stupendous proportion, but, nevertheless, was finished in a masterful, scientific and scholarly manner by Mr. Nitchie. A review of the original edition reveals an uncanny ability on the part of the writer to utilize the most progressive methods used in the teaching of reading today.

Modern scientific methods of education have also been employed in the complete revision of the text made by Elizabeth Helm Nitchie and Gertrude Torrey, both thoroughly capable Nitchie School teachers of vast and successful experience. This revision was undertaken to bring the original reading exercises up to date and to include new methods of teaching which have proved to be effective.

One of the most wholesome and most inspiring messages is to be found in the chapter "To the Friends of the Deaf." An acceptance of the philosophy presented in this chapter would add much to the sum total of happiness for the hard-of-hearing and their friends. It not only offers hope, but supplies a specific program. At the same time it encourages the friends of the deaf to develop not only a thoughtful attitude, but above all a sympathetic understanding.

The lessons are based on a collection of stories that are unmatched for joy and good humor. It would be absolutely impossible to conduct a class, using these stories as a basis, without creating an atmosphere of good cheer and friendliness. When a course of lessons maintains such an optimistic atmosphere, a long step has been made in solving the hard-of-hearing teaching problem.

The revised edition has not only provided for the creation of the correct mental attitude on the part of the students, but it has provided for ample systematic drill, and has laid emphasis on drill where emphasis is necessary. The section on colloquial sentences, for example, reminds one of present-day language texts

INTRODUCTION

which provide opportunities for drills in varied situations. The topics include such up-to-date subjects as radio, bridge, golf, movies and the stock market.

All recognize that at best the spoken language is not well adapted to the purpose of lip-reading. Instead of literally throwing up their hands at this situation, the author and those revising the book have placed great emphasis upon the necessity of mastering, absolutely and perfectly, the easier lip movements in order that one's synthetic powers may be utilized fully in the more complex and difficult situations.

One of the characteristic features of the modern project method of teaching is that the situations provided for in the school should be essentially the same as those found in life. The methods included in this book follow this modern idea by showing the necessity of teaching and learning the movements of the lips made in speaking at an ordinary rate. Emphasis is placed on special and individual sounds and on word drill, but the complete thought or sentence is considered the unit rather than individual words or sounds.

Lip-reading is for the imaginative, but can

be mastered by anyone who has the attitude of "I can and I will." This revised edition, with its many helpful suggestions, will be very helpful to those who cannot receive actual class instruction.

The hard-of-hearing owe a great debt to Edward B. Nitchie, Elizabeth Helm Nitchie and Gertrude Torrey. How well they would feel repaid if more unfortunate individuals could but be made to realize how much joy and satisfaction awaits them if they will only avail themselves of the service which this monumental work affords.

JOHN A. STEVENSON.

CONTENTS

	PAGE
INTRODUCTION—DR. JOHN A. STEVENSON	ix
FOREWORD—ELIZABETH H. NITCHIE	xv

PART I
FOR THE STUDENT AND HIS FRIENDS

TO THE FRIENDS OF THE DEAF	1
THE EYE AS A SUBSTITUTE FOR DEAF EARS	14

PART II
LESSON MATERIAL

HOW TO USE STORIES	27
STORIES FOR PRACTISE	38
LESSONS ON THE MOVEMENTS	85
Consonants Formed and Revealed by the Lips	100
Extended Vowels	101
Consonants Formed and Revealed by the Lips (Cont.)	107
Relaxed Vowels	110
Consonants Formed by the Tongue and Revealed by the Lips	116
Double Consonants	124
Puckered Vowels	128

CONTENTS

Consonants Formed and Revealed by the Tongue 135
   Double Consonants 143
   Diphthongs with Puckered Final Movement 146
Consonants Revealed by Context 152
   Double Consonants 158
Diphthongs (Cont.) 160
COLLOQUIAL FORMS, VOWEL AND CONSONANT EXERCISES AND HOMOPHENOUS WORDS 166
   Lessons on Colloquial Forms, Vowel and Consonant Exercises and Homophenous Words 180
LESSONS ON VARIATIONS OF FUNDAMENTAL MOVEMENTS AND UNACCENTED VOWELS 265
COLLOQUIAL SENTENCES 291
PROVERBS 313
ADDITIONAL HOMOPHENOUS WORDS 318

PART III
FOR THE TEACHER

FOR THE TEACHER 325
   General Principles 327
   Teaching Aims 330
   Giving the Lesson 339
   Lesson Outlines 346

APPENDICES

A TABLE OF VOWELS AND DIPHTHONGS . . . 362
B TABLE OF CONSONANTS 365
C BIBLIOGRAPHY 366

FOREWORD

When "Lip-Reading Principles and Practise" came from the press eighteen years ago it was welcomed by teachers as an up-to-date method of teaching lip-reading, and as a forward-looking text-book on the subject that would change methods then in use. Mr. Nitchie's well-trained mind, his unusual understanding of the psychology and pedagogy of teaching reading and foreign languages, and his patience in working out the details of his system made possible the production of this text-book. To quote from Miss Elizabeth Brand's "Aftermath," a tribute to Mr. Nitchie published in the "Volta Review" in December, 1917:

"The perspicacity of the teacher's mind was equalled by its depth, its grasp of detail, and its activity. He probed for knowledge; he classified, and systematized, and simplified; then he kept on growing and giving. 'Better go backward than not to move,' he said.

"His great contribution to the teaching art

has been the making of lip-reading instruction psycho-physiological. The teaching of lip-reading had been, up to his time, a physiological process; he made it a mental process. What many psychologists, working together, have done for the pedagogy of reading, Nitchie has done for the pedagogy of lip-reading.

"The system of lip-reading embodied in his text-book is delightful because of its logical development, simplicity of treatment, and a vein of humor which makes pleasant what would otherwise be tedious. But Mr. Nitchie always laid emphasis upon methods rather than system; his teachers were instructed in methods, could choose their own system if they liked, and were given latitude for growth."

"Lip-Reading Principles and Practise" was not the first but the fourth of Mr. Nitchie's text-books, each new book taking the place of the one previously published. He did not claim to have discovered new principles, only to have adapted well-known principles of psychology and pedagogy to his particular subject.

Even after eighteen years have passed we cannot find changes that need to be made in the methods; but experience in using the text-book has shown the need for further simplification and development along certain lines to make the book easier to use by teachers generally. The sequence of lesson material, as it is presented in this revision, is the order decided upon by Mr. Nitchie himself after using the book with his students. He believed that teachers should give original sentences and prepare much of the material themselves, adapting it to the requirements of different types of students and their interests, so sentences had not been written for all of the lessons. Many teachers have found this a drawback in using the book, and students have not had complete lesson material for home practise. Therefore, this revision provides sentences for all lessons, and instructions and explanations have been simplified.

Dr. John A. Stevenson, an educator and lecturer of note and the author of "The Project Method of Teaching," and other books, urged me to undertake the revision, believing it would make possible a much wider use of the text-book by teachers of lip-reading in colleges and private and public schools. He was kind enough to tell me wherein he found the book difficult to use, though himself an expert in teaching methods. We are deeply indebted to him for his suggestions and for his willingness to put his stamp of approval upon what we have done.

So many have contributed in one way or another to the revising of "Lip-Reading Principles and Practise" that it would be impossible to mention each one by name. Often it was a criticism or suggestion from a student or fellow teacher that started a train of thought leading to a change. Professor George Burton Hotchkiss, Chairman of the Department of Marketing, and Professor of Advertising and Business English at New York University, was particularly helpful in his suggestions, and I wish to express my appreciation of his kindness, his interest in all that concerned the school, and his willingness to help.

Before beginning the work of revision a letter was sent to all of Mr. Nitchie's normal graduates asking for suggestions, and the responses were gratifying and helpful. There were many suggestions made that we could use; others that were helpful because they started us thinking along new lines, and still others that were excellent in themselves but that could not be fitted into the scheme of things. All were appreciated, and grateful acknowledgment is made to each and every one who responded.

We wish especially to make acknowledgment to the Misses Mary Pauline Ralli and Kathryn Alling of The Nitchie School of Lip-Reading for their valuable criticisms and suggestions, and for testing much of the material with their students. Miss Mary V. Carney, Principal of the school, gave the fullest coöperation. It was Miss Alling who suggested the arrangement of the lessons on Colloquial Forms, Vowel and Consonant Exercises, and Homophenous Words. Miss Ralli wrote the colloquial sentences on Music and provided other groups. Miss Coralie N. Kenfield of San Francisco tested the material with the students in her public school classes, and gave us the benefit of criticisms and suggestions. The table of vowel sounds in the explanatory material preceding Lessons on the Movements was adapted from the notes she uses with her students, and use was made of other notes that she so generously lent us. Miss M. Faircloth of Toronto also has been most generous in offering the use of her notes for a first lesson that we have embodied in the instructions for teachers. She, too, made helpful criticisms and suggestions. Mrs. Florence M. Evans of Eugene, Oregon, revised stories and supplied some of the new ones. Miss Jane B. Walker of New York was kind enough to give us the benefit of her unusual training as a teacher and lecturer, and to write the colloquial sentences on Art. Mrs. Joseph F. Block of Laurel, Miss., contributed sentences on Golf; Mrs. Frank S. Berger, those on Bridge.

But it is to the Master, Edward B. Nitchie, to whom we owe the inspiration and the training that made it possible for us to go forward with the work which he laid down in October, 1917. We have tried to be true to his principles, to change only where change was clearly indicated, without disturbing the logical development of his system; to make more definitely his the system and methods he had contributed to the teaching of lip-reading, and to give them a larger and more lasting place in the educational field.

ELIZABETH HELM NITCHIE
(MRS. EDWARD B. NITCHIE)

October 1, 1930

Part I
FOR THE STUDENT AND HIS FRIENDS

CHAPTER I

TO THE FRIENDS OF THE DEAF

It is not easy to be deaf; it is a mighty hard thing; and it is often made harder for us by the unnecessary friction between us and our friends arising from the fact of our deafness. That is why I ask you, the friends of the deaf, to consider some of the ways and means by which you can help to make our lot easier for us. I do not mean to scold or find fault, but to help—to help you to help us. If at times I speak plainly, even bluntly, I trust you will pardon it in view of my purpose.

If it is a question of blame, we ourselves must assume our share of it. It is often our attitude that makes things hard for both you and us. For one thing, we are prone to be too sensitive. And yet that is the most natural thing in the world. I suppose every man or woman who carries a physical affliction is more or less sensitive. The lame man, the blind man, the humpback, the stammerer, all have a fellow feeling in this regard. But the peculiarity of deafness is that it has the unhappy faculty of drawing down ridicule upon its victim.

If a lame man stumbles and falls, nobody laughs; everybody rushes to help him to his feet. If a blind man runs into a stone wall, every one is all sympathy. But let a deaf man make a mistake, due to his deafness, and everybody laughs. Yes, I know they do not laugh at him; they laugh at his mistake. If it were only easy for him to realize that, it would save him intense mortification. I suppose there is not one of us who has not felt at some time or other that he wished the floor would open and swallow him up.

When I was at college, one of the members of the glee club was very bald; but he wore a wig. At the concerts he sang a solo:

> "I'd rather have fingers than toes,
> I'd rather have eyes than a nose;
> And as for my hair,
> I'm so glad it's all there,
> I'll be sore as can be when it goes."

And with the last word he would snatch the wig from his head. Of course everybody laughed; but the point is, that *he laughed with them*. If we who are deaf would cultivate the saving grace of laughing at our mistakes, it would take all the sting out of them.

On the other hand, there is the danger that those who laugh at us may get the worst of it themselves. John Wanamaker tells the story of a deaf man named Brown, who was disposed to stinginess.

"He never married, but he was very fond of society, so one day he felt compelled to give a banquet to the many ladies and gentlemen whose guest he had been.

"They were amazed that his purse-strings had been unloosed so far, and they thought he deserved encouragement; so it was arranged that he should be toasted. One of the most daring young men of the company was selected, for it took a lot of nerve to frame and propose a toast to so unpopular a man as Miser Brown. But the young man rose. And this is what was heard by every one except Brown, who never heard anything that was not roared into his ear:

"'Here's to you, Miser Brown. You are no better than a tramp, and it is suspected that you got most of your money dishonestly.

We trust that you may get your just deserts yet, and land in the penitentiary.'

"Visible evidences of applause made Brown smile with gratification. He got upon his feet, raised his glass to his lips, and said, 'The same to you, sir.'"

Inattention is one of our chief faults. Not hearing what is going on around us, we are apt to withdraw into our own thoughts; and then, when some one does speak to us, we are far away. We need to be more on the alert than others, just because we cannot hear; our quickness of eye must make up for our aural slowness. To you, our friends, I wish to make the suggestion that you draw our attention, not by touching us, not by a violent waving of the arm or perhaps the handkerchief, not by shouting to us, but by a quiet movement of the hand within our range of vision. We are sensitive. Anything that brings our affliction into the limelight of the observation of others cuts like a lash; and there are few things we dislike more than having our attention attracted by a poke or a pull, though a gentle touch is sometimes not disagreeable.

Another of our faults is a tendency to seclusiveness. We not only draw into our own thoughts when others are present; we often retire from company into the solitude of a book or magazine, or avoid company altogether. It is a rudeness, I know, to pick up a book and read when in the company of others; yet it is a rudeness that even our friends ought sympathetically to condone. And, moreover, I ask you which is the greater rudeness, that of our taking up our book or that of your passing around the sweets of conversation and offering none to us? Truly, we ought not to seclude ourselves, but we need your help.

We have our faults, and so have you, and your chief fault, as far as we are concerned, is that you do not realize what it means to be deaf. Occasionally I hear some one say he wishes he might be deaf for a little while; he would be glad if some of the disturbing noises might be eliminated. Oh, deafness is not so bad, he opines; it has its advantages— which I do not deny; but they are not the advantages he has in mind. I sometimes wish that such a person might truly be deaf for say a year without the knowledge that at the end of that time his hearing would be restored to him. Then he would find the one-time disturbing noises had become music in his ears, and that the advantages of deafness, provided he had met his affliction in the right spirit, were of a spiritual and not of a physical nature.

It is thoughtlessness, due to ignorance of conditions, that is the cause of most of the troubles between you and us. It is not selfishness—not usually, at any rate—but just that you do not stop to think. And that is why I am writing to you: to help you to understand and show the same thoughtfulness toward us as you instinctively would show toward the blind.

There is one book that every friend of the deaf ought to read, "Deafness and Cheerfulness,"* by the Rev. A. W. Jackson. Intended for the deaf themselves, it has a still greater value, I believe, for their friends. The little brochure, "The Deaf in Art and the Art of Being Deaf," by Grace Ellery Channing, is also good. Such reading will help you to put yourselves in our place.

It is easy enough for us to imagine what lameness and what blindness mean; probably most of us have been more or less lame at some time or other, and we are all of us blind

* This book is out-of-print.

when in the dark. But it is a much more difficult thing for the hearing to imagine the full calamity of deafness. Think how much of the sweetness of life comes to you through your ears. The joys of companionship and fellowship with other men and women are dependent on our understanding what they have to say. Try for one week to imagine what it would be like if every spoken word that comes to you were lost. Think each time, "Suppose I had not heard that," and when you have finally comprehended what the world of silence is, your sympathetic understanding will go a long way toward lightening our cross.

If you could really put yourselves in our place, one of the first things you would realize is that there are few things that so irritate as to have you shout at us. It is so unnecessary and uncalled for, and makes us the center of unenvied observation. We will in fact understand you better if instead of shouting you enunciate clearly and distinctly and make your voice as vibrant as may be possible.

In a general conversation we greatly need your help. A certain deaf man expressed the unuttered view of many another when he said, "I enjoy a conversation with one person, but when a third breaks in upon us, h—— enters the room with him." In nine cases out of ten the deaf man is given no share in general conversation, and for all purposes of social enjoyment he might almost as well be marooned on a desert island.

General conversation is hard for us to understand, even though we be skillful readers of the lips. As we all know, it is very much easier to follow conversation when we know the subject. When two people are talking we may say that each has a one-half share; when three, each has a one-third share, and so on. This is true provided all can hear. But if one is deaf, while it is still true he has a half-share when only two are talking, when three are talking he has no share at all! If only the others would talk to him! But no, they talk to each other, and he is out of it. My advice to you, then, in a general conversation, is: "Talk to us." The others will hear you, and it will give us the benefit of sharing in the conversation, of knowing the subject, and of greatly increased ease of understanding.

There are times, I know, when it is not

possible to talk to us, or others may be talking who have not the thoughtfulness to do so. Then what we ask of you is not to rehash the conversation after the topic has been talked out, but by a word or two at the beginning to indicate to us the subject.

The suggestions I have given you so far will apply whether we are lip-readers or not. Now I wish to give you some suggestions that will help us in our endeavor to hear with the eyes. For one thing, let the light be on your face, not on ours. It requires only a little thoughtfulness to see to this important requisite. In my own family such thoughtfulness has become so instinctive as to be a habit, and the endeavor to get the light right is always a first thought when any of the family are talking to me.

The exaggeration of the facial movements, "mouthing," usually arises on your part from the best intentions to help us understand. You mean well, but as a matter of fact you are making it harder for us. Such exaggeration throws the mouth out of all natural movement and formation, and makes it impossible for us to know just what we do see. All we ask of you is that you speak distinctly, and then the movements of your lips and tongue will take care of themselves.

Closely associated with your endeavor to help us by exaggeration is the endeavor to help through a word-by-word manner of talking. The human mind naturally takes in the thought as a whole and not piecemeal, one word at a time. It is exasperation to ask us to understand in that way. How much of the thought of this printed page would you get if you stopped to think about each word separately? Like the man who could not see the woods for the trees, so when—you—talk—this—way we cannot see the thought for the words. If it is necessary to speak slowly to us, let it be smoothly, connectedly, and not word by word.

Another of your well-meant efforts to help us consists in repeating for us a single word that we have failed to understand; it is much easier for us to get the word in its thought connection in a sentence. For the same reason, the long phrase is usually easier than the short phrase; as, for example, "Will you get me a drink of water?" presents much less difficulty than "Will you get me a drink?"

In your choice of words, try to choose if possible those that have the most movement of the lips. If you want to say "a quarter," choose the words "twenty-five cents." For "fifty cents," however, you should say "half a dollar," for not only does the latter phrase have more lip-movement, but it is also true that "fifty cents" might easily be mistaken for "fifteen cents." As another example, notice as you say the sentences how much plainer and more pronounced the lip-movements are for "What beautiful weather we are having" than for "Isn't it a nice day?"

Proper names are always hard, because we have as a rule no context to help us. When you introduce us to strangers, be careful to speak the name clearly and distinctly direct to us. Not infrequently I find my hearing friends introducing me with a decided emphasis on my own name, as though it were very necessary that I should understand that, and with the name of my new acquaintance so mumbled that I do not know whether he is Teufelsdröckh or Smith. Again, when in conversation you are referring to some one by name, a short explanatory phrase will often help us wonderfully; as, "I like to deal at Scudder and Singer's—*the meat market, you know.*"

I have presented to you some of our problems, believing that you can help us. Yet I realize that you cannot do it all—that we must coöperate. And the first thing for us to do in the way of self-help is frankly to acknowledge our deafness. I think no greater mistake can be made from the standpoint of our own comfort and peace of mind than that of trying to conceal the fact that we cannot hear. It is not only sensitiveness, it is also a feeling of shame, as though we had done some wrong, that impels us to try to hide our failing ears. We need the advice of the lunatic in the story. All day long a fisherman had been sitting on the bank of the stream and had not caught a thing. All day long the lunatic had watched him from a window in the neighboring insane asylum. At last the man in the window could endure it no longer, and he shouted to the fisherman: "Hey, there, you poor fool! Come on inside!"

So we need to come on inside the ranks to which we belong, frankly, realizing that it is no crime to be deaf, and then try by every means in our power to make our lives normal and sane. That is what we are striving to do, and we ask your help that our burden of deafness may be lightened as much as possible.

CHAPTER II

THE EYE AS A SUBSTITUTE FOR DEAF EARS

It is well known that the blind in a measure substitute hearing for sight; sounds of traffic in a busy street are a confused roar to the untrained ear, but to the experienced blind man they are a fairly reliable guide on his way.

Even to a greater degree can the deaf man train his eye to substitute for his deaf ears.

Watch the mouth of anyone who is speaking, and you will see many clearly defined movements of the lips, perhaps even of the tongue. The eye trained to associate certain movements with certain sounds has the power of interpreting these movements into words and sentences.

A very large percentage of the deaf are, I believe, incurable, at least at the present state of medical and surgical knowledge. The greatest loss to anyone who is deaf is the loss of understanding speech. Inability to hear music or the voices of nature is a deprivation; but inability to hear spoken language is a calamity, unless other means than the ear can be found to convey the message to the brain; for in the ability to understand spoken language lies the way not only to the pleasures of life, but to the truest necessities of the soul and body.

Deafness is a physical bar to employment second only to blindness, and bears especially heavily on the man who, dependent on others for his salary, becomes deaf in adult life. Lip-reading, or speech-reading, "that subtile art," as Dr. John Bulwer said in 1648, "which may inable one with an Observant Eie to Heare what any man Speaks by the moving of his Lips," is a valuable substitute for hearing, as far as spoken language is concerned, though, like any other substitutes, it has its limitations. By it the sense of sight is forced to interpret a medium for expressing thought which, throughout the history of the race, has been developed for the needs of the sense of hearing. I shall show later how imperfectly spoken language is fitted to the requirements of successful lip-reading.

The problem of the teacher varies according to the class of the deaf to which his pupil belongs, for the deaf-mute's needs are only in part the needs of the hard-of-hearing. My work lies with the hard-of-hearing—and by that term I mean those who, either partly or totally deaf, became so after having acquired speech and language—and it is of their problem of which I shall speak particularly. It is not only their problem; its solution becomes also the solution of the problem of the deaf-mute *after* he acquires speech and language.

The problem of teaching lip-reading is truly a psychological problem. Both the eyes and the mind must be trained, but mind-training is the more important factor.

The difficulties for the eyes to overcome are two: first, the obscurity of many of the movements, and second, the rapidity of their formation. That spoken language is not well adapted to the purpose of lip-reading is evident from the many sounds that are formed within the mouth or even in the throat. The difference between vocal and non-vocal consonants is invisible to the eye. The aspirate *h*, as in "hat," cannot be seen; there is no visible difference between "hat" and "at." The consonants formed by the back of the tongue and soft palate, *k*, hard *g*, *ng*, are seldom revealed to the eye of the lip-reader; likewise, certain tongue consonants, as *t, d, n,* and *y*, present almost insuperable difficulties. Double tongue consonants, as *nt, nd, lt, ld,* are also just as indefinite and obscure in their visible formation.

Rapidity of the movements is another serious difficulty in the way of successful lip-reading. From one-twelfth to one-thirteenth of a second is the average time per movement in ordinary speech. This is the average, but some movements are of course slower, while others, particularly those for unaccented syllables, are much quicker.

With such difficulties as these, the wonder is that anyone can read the lips at all. Eye-training can never eliminate them, though it can lessen them in a measure. The method should aim first always to study or see the movements in words or sentences, not formed singly by themselves. Sounds pronounced singly all tend to be exaggerated, and many of them even to be grossly mispronounced. Moreover, one movement often modifies decidedly the appearance of another connected with it in a word. For example, long *e* usually tends to show a slight drawing back of the corners of the mouth, as in "thief;" but, after *sh,* as in "sheep," this is scarcely visible.

In the second place the method should aim always to study or see the movements as the words are pronounced quickly. It is true that it would be easier to see them when spoken slowly, but it is also true that to produce the best results the eye should be trained from the first to see things as they must always be seen in ordinary speech, and that is rapidly.

And, in the third place, the method should aim to inculcate a nearly infallible accuracy and quickness of perception of the easier movements, leaving to the mind in large measure the task of supplying the harder movements.

With the eye thus trained it often happens that the lip-reader's impression is that of actually hearing what is said. If I put the tubes of a phonograph into my ears, so that I can hear every word, and close my eyes, unbidden and without conscious effort the vision of the moving lips of the speaker forming the flow of the words passes before my mind.

Although it is not possible for the eye to see each and every movement, it is possible for the mind to grasp a complete impression without even the consciousness that it has "supplied" so many of the movements and sounds. The chief difficulties in the way of the mind in lip-reading may be indicated by describing that type of mind which is uniformly most successful, and that is a mind which is quick to respond to impressions, or quick in its reaction time, and a mind in which the synthetic qualities are dominant. The difficulties, then, are to overcome the opposite conditions or tendencies, and the aim is to develop the mind to the utmost along the line of these favoring conditions.

Fortunately thought is quicker than speech. Testing myself with a selected passage that I know by heart it takes me fifteen seconds to think of it word by word, and thirty-five seconds to read it aloud. To develop quick perception, *practise* is the essential; that is, slow speech, word-by-word utterance, must be avoided, and all forms of exercise must be given to the pupil up to the limit of speed which his ability will allow. This undoubtedly makes the work harder for the time being, but it results in more rapid progress.

Not only is thought quicker than speech;

thought need not formulate every word to have clear conceptions. Thought skips; thought looks ahead and anticipates. So that a correct understanding of an idea is possible without a word-for-word accuracy. That is the way the baby understands what is said to him. I would say to my little boy, when a year and a half old, "How does daddy shave himself in the morning?" That he understood every word was not possible; probably "daddy" and "shave" were the only ones he really knew. But that he understood what I said he made evident when he went through the motion of shaving his own face with his finger.

The method of mind-training should aim to develop this power of grasping thoughts as wholes, and to avoid strictly anything that will enhance the opposite tendency of demanding verbal accuracy before anything is understood at all. Minds of the latter type are literal, analytical, unimaginative. Yet there are very few who are altogether of this kind; most of us, however analytical, have some synthetic powers, some ability of putting things together, of constructing the whole from the parts, of quick intuition. It is by developing these powers that real success in lip-reading can be attained, and it is by working along these lines that the surest way is found in the end to the understanding of every word. Even those who hear, often have an experience like this: Some one will make a remark which you fail to understand; the word "what" is on your lips, but before it is fairly uttered the whole sentence will come to you like a flash. When this intuitive, synthetic power is highly developed, the "natural-born" lip-reader is the result.

I feel sure, from what is known of the men, that Prescott, the historian, would have easily learned lip-reading, while the analytical Bancroft would have found it much more difficult; that Seton Thompson would be quick to master it, and that John Burroughs would be slower; that Roosevelt would be an expert, and that Hughes would be a novice. I have repeatedly found among my pupils that those who can play music readily at sight are apt in reading the lips, for such ability implies quick reaction time and the intuitive mind.

What degree of skill can a lip-reader expect to attain? How long does it take? These are natural questions, but cannot be answered categorically. What some can attain in three months, others cannot acquire short of a year; and the highest degree of skill, as in any art, is open only to the few. But three lessons a week for three months will, with most pupils, give a very satisfactory and practical skill. I may be pardoned if I speak of myself. I can sometimes understand a lecture or sermon, depending upon conditions of light, etc.; less often can I understand a play. I am called a good lip-reader, but I know better ones. With a very few exceptions, such a degree of skill is possible to every one as to make home life and social friendships a joy once more, and, though it may not be an infallible resource in business, it may for all be an invaluable aid. Lip-reading can never do all that good ears ought to do, but what it can do is almost a miracle.

Two objections to lip-reading I occasionally hear: (1) That it is too great a strain on the eyes, and (2) that, by relieving the ears from hearing, there is a tendency to deterioration in hearing from lack of exercise.

The strain upon the eyes at first is truly no small one; but I have repeatedly found that those who complain of eye-strain during their first lessons, later never think any more about it. I have not strong eyes, and now, though I use them in reading the lips every day and all day long, they are seldom over-tired. If the lip-reader is careful from the first to cease using the eyes at the first symptom of tire, I believe that no harm can result and gradually the eyes will be able to do more and more.

The objection in regard to the deterioration of hearing I believe to be the reverse of true. Dr. Albert Barnes, in "The Dietetic and Hygienic Gazette," of October, 1909, said: "People with ear-strain should spare the hearing as much as possible, and, instead of straining the ear to catch what is said, they should watch the lips more. In other words, the eyes should be called upon to help the ears." Moreover, with pupils who have enough hearing to hear the sound of the voice, I advise and encourage them to use ears and eyes in fullest coöperation, one helping the other.

Under such circumstances, and also in view of the fact that the ear involuntarily gets exercise with every sound that comes to it, whether the strain to hear is made or not, I do not see how any harm can be done to the ears by lip-reading, and in all my experience I have never found any evidence of such harm. On the contrary, several times pupils have reported to me an actual betterment of the hearing, though how much lip-reading had to do with it and how much other conditions I do not pretend to say.

Lip-reading, then, is not a cure for deafness, nor is it even a cure for all the ills of deafness; but from some of the worst ills it is a true alleviation. It takes first place on the majority of occasions over all mechanical devices. For those completely deaf, or so deaf as to make mechanical devices out of the question, lip-reading is the only resource. For those whose deafness still allows them to hear the sound of the voice, it obviates the necessity of using these more or less cumbersome and inconvenient contrivances. Even at such times when these devices can be used to advantage, watching the lips helps to make them more useful and more reliable. Under any circumstances, lip-reading has in it the power to make deafness of whatever degree much easier to bear.

Part II
LESSON MATERIAL

HOW TO USE STORIES

To know how to use the stories and other reading matter for practise we must know why we use them. There is such a thing as practising in the wrong way. In spite of the opinion held by some that "just practise" is all that is necessary, it is not so much the *amount* of practise as it is the *kind* of practise that produces the best results. There are right and wrong ways of doing everything, and in lip-reading it is possible to practise in a way that will do absolute harm. One hour of the right kind of practise is worth five hours of the wrong kind.

Keep in mind that the aim of all practise is to acquire skill in understanding *conversation*. In ordinary conversation people talk rapidly. No lip-reader, however skilful, can be absolutely sure of seeing every word. But he can be sure of understanding all the thought, even though words be lost.

The best lip-readers are invariably those who have the power of grasping the thought as a whole, and not through a word-by-word deciphering of the sentence. And, in the end, the surest way of understanding practically every word is not through a word-by-word method, but it is through developing this synthetic power of constructing the whole from the parts. That is, if the whole thought is understood, the visual memory of the rest of the sentence will most surely and usually subconsciously supply the missing words.

Care must be taken, however, to see that in an effort to train for thought-wholes and for quick thought-getting, the student does not get the wrong thought, or jump to the wrong conclusions from the few words seen. The student cheats himself by "bluffing" or pretending that he understands when he does not. He should not interrupt in the middle of a sentence, for if he waits until it is completed he may get the whole sentence "in a flash." But he should not allow himself to lose the thread of the story.

The chief value of the stories and reading matter as material for practise lies in their use for developing the synthetic qualities mentioned. To develop the right habits of mind, and the mental attitude that is quickest to understand conversation, stories are invaluable.

Because the student is being trained in *habits of mind,* he should use the stories in a way that will build the right habits. It is extremely difficult for some minds to see thought-wholes. The fact that one student may get a thought quickly, and so understand the stories readily, and another may have difficulty with the stories, does not indicate that one student is more brilliant than another. It merely shows that the minds of the two students work in different ways.

The way to overcome the difficulties of the analytical mind is not to allow a slow, word-by-word understanding, but, rather, to make use of the help of memory. Some students are enabled to read thought-wholes from the lips if they have read over the material before the lesson. Far better to make use of memory-help and train the mind to work in the right way, than not to use it and build up bad habits.

When practising the stories at home, the student should have someone read the story to him in a tone so low that he cannot hear any of the words. First, however, the assistant should read the story to himself to gain familiarity with it, and then in reading to the student, should read it as he would talk, that is, in the colloquial, rather than the recitative style. The student should interrupt if he does not get the thought of every sentence, and every clause. In which case the whole sentence or whole clause should be repeated. He should not interrupt for every word. It is necessary to train the mind in the habit of grasping the whole from the parts, and there is no better way for a beginner to do it than by using stories in this manner. If after two or three trials the student cannot get the sentence, the assistant should express the thought in other words, or give a clue word, or show the sentence, and should then repeat the sentence.

After the story has been read for the thought, the assistant should tell the story in his own words. Let him add detail and give as much change in the wording as he can. "A lesson in Physiology," (Story No. 16, p. 47) is thus changed as an example:

A teacher was talking to her pupils about the different organs of the body. She told them that an organ of the body is a special part of the body. And she told them very carefully about the eyes, and the ears, the nose, the mouth, and the hand. And then, after she had told them all about it, she wanted to find out how much they remembered, so she asked them. But nobody replied.

"Oh," she said, "I am sure some of you must know what an organ of the body is. Come now, all who know raise your hands."

The smallest boy in the room put his hand up. "I know, teacher," he said.

"Well, tell us then," said the teacher. "What is an organ of the body?"

And the boy replied: "I smell with my nose-organ, I see with my eye-organ, I hear with my ear-organ, I eat with my mouth-organ, and I feel with my hand-organ."

The student should try to grasp the sentence, or the thought, as a whole. He should not repeat after the assistant; but interrupt at the end of a sentence if he fails to understand. Perhaps at first the changed wording may be more difficult than the original story, with which he is familiar. But in time he will find the assistant's own wording easier than the original form, for it is easier. And if he is really reading the lips and not simply following from memory of the words, he ought to understand the colloquial form better than the written.

The next step in practising the story at home

is to have the assistant ask questions on the story. Questions are an important part of conversation. Practise in answering questions, therefore, is essential. The questions should be natural, and at first rather simple. The words and phrases of the story may well be re-used if they make a *natural* question. It is better not to have many questions that can be answered by yes or no, as the assistant cannot be sure the questions have been understood.

The questions should not be repeated after the assistant, as that would require a word-by-word understanding of it. Such an understanding is not necessary in order to answer a great many questions; if a few words suggesting the thought be grasped, the question can be answered intelligently. In ordinary conversation this is true over and over again, and therefore the lip-reader should seek to cultivate this mental attitude toward the questions. In this practise work with the assistant, the question should be answered if the thought is understood.

A few questions based on "A Lesson in Physiology" are given as examples:

What was the teacher explaining to her class? What did she tell them an organ of the body is? What examples did she give them? What did she want to find out, after she had told them all about it? How long before she had a reply? Who raised his hand at last? What did he say he saw with? What did he smell with? What did he do with his mouth organ? How did he feel?

While it is true that the chief value of the stories lies in their use for developing mental habits, it is also true that valuable training for the eyes can be gained through mirror practise. Mirror practise is a stumbling block to many students because they do not understand either its purpose or the correct method to be used.

The mirror is a true aid in the study of lip reading if it be used in the right way. It is possible to use the mirror in such way as to waste time—or even worse, in such way as to do positive harm. It is common to hear a student of lip-reading say: "I do not get any good from mirror practise; I know just what I am saying." If such as these only knew it, that is exactly why mirror practise should prove helpful.

We must keep in mind the purpose of mirror practise. Lip-reading as an art comprises fundamentally two different kinds of skill:

(1) the ability to recognize quickly the sound and word formations as shown by the visible organs of speech, and (2) the ability to grasp the thought of the speaker. Mirror practise is not at all intended to develop the second kind of skill; it is obviously impossible to have any practise in understanding thought by watching our own mouths in the mirror; but as a means of training the eye to know and to recognize quickly the sound and word formations, mirror practise has a peculiar value *just because the student knows what he is saying,* for thus he never makes a mistake; he always associates the right movement with the right sound. Really to know the movements, they must be so learned that their recognition becomes a habit; that is, something that the mind does without conscious effort. In forming such a habit it is not only essential that the desired association should be made over and over again, but also that there should be no false associations.

But to make mirror practise thus valuable it must be done in the right way. To say words and sentences before the mirror and watch the mouth for everything in general and nothing in particular is a waste of time. Mirror practise must be definite if it is to have value. It is so easy to let the mind wander, to make only vague associations, that we might just as well not practise with the mirror at all unless we can find a way to fix our attention definitely and in detail upon the thing we are looking for.

A still worse evil than vagueness in connection with mirror practise arises from mouthing or exaggeration of the movements, and sometimes from mistaken pronunciations or false formations of them. To mouth or exaggerate is to give us wrong ideas of the sound and word formations, which is not simply a waste of time, but also tends to lead us astray when reading the lips of others.

One of the values gained from mirror practise, that is often overlooked, is from *feeling* the formation of the sounds as they are repeated. When practising with the mirror be sure to use voice, and to think of the motor sensations of the words or movements as they are repeated.

The method of sentence practise with the mirror, whether working with the stories, or sentences in other lesson material, is to take a short sentence, or a complete clause if the sentence is long, and *say the sentence, or clause, as many times as there are words in it,* each time concentrating on a different word, one word at a time. The first time say the entire sentence, or clause, *naturally,* and concentrate on the first word, the second time on the second word, and so on. The student should be careful not to emphasize the word for which he is looking. Then the student should repeat the sentence, or clause, thinking of the motor sensations of the words.

Sentences are to be practised with the mirror for the study of the word formations that make up the sentence, and one of the particular values is to get the effect of the unaccented vowels.

Bear in mind that mirror practise has only a certain value; it is not the chief value to be gained from the stories. Give only a few minutes at a time to it, for it is monotonous and the mind quickly wanders. It is far better to have ten or fifteen minutes of concentrated practise than to spend a much longer period on it when the mind is constantly wandering to other things.

As has been pointed out, the aim of this practise is to train for a *subconscious* knowledge of the movements. Therefore, the results

HOW TO USE STORIES

will not be seen, except in a more accurate reading of the lips. Whether or not the student is aware of the benefits gained from mirror practise, it will help in the end, provided it is done in the right way.

The things to avoid are vagueness, which is a waste of time, and false associations, which are a positive harm. The things to be sought are definiteness and correct associations through hearing, feeling and seeing the sounds and movements.

STORIES FOR PRACTISE

Of Course

1. It was little Mary's first day at school. Her name had been registered, and the teacher asked:

"Have you any brothers and sisters?"

"Yes, ma'am," answered Mary.

"Are you the oldest one in the family?"

"Oh, no, ma'am," said Mary, "father and mother's both older than me."

—*"Make 'Em Laugh Again"—by Lurie.**

The Last Speaker

2. A man had been invited to speak at a Conference but the chairman introduced several speakers who were not on the program and the audience was tired out when he finally presented the last speaker, saying, "Mr. Jones will now give his address."

"My address," said Mr. Jones, bowing, "is

---

* Stories from *"Make 'Em Laugh Again"* by Lurie are used through the courtesy of G. P. Putnam's Sons.

number one hundred and fifty-seven Broadway, and I wish you all goodnight!"

Is Your Mother Home?

3. One day as little Jimmie was sitting upon some steps, a man came over to him and said, "Little boy, is your mother at home?"

"Yes, sir," was the reply.

The man rang the bell, but no one answered. He rang again, but still no one answered. After ringing a third time he turned to Jimmie impatiently and said, "I thought you said that your mother was at home?"

"She is," was the prompt reply, "but I don't live here."

Unanswerable

4. A teacher was giving a lesson on the circulation of the blood. Trying to make the matter clearer, he said: "Now, boys, if I stood on my head the blood, as you know, would run into it, and I should turn red in the face."

"Yes, sir," said the boys.

"Then why is it that while I am standing upright in the ordinary position the blood doesn't run into my feet?"

A little fellow shouted, "'Cause yer feet ain't empty!"

—"The Best Stories in the World." Masson.*

Friendly Relations

5. A little girl was lost on the street, and was brought into the police station. The officers tried in every way to learn her name. Finally, one of the officers said:

"Tell me, little girl, what name does your mother call your father?"

"Why," responded the child innocently, "she doesn't call him any names; she likes him."

—"The Best Stories in the World." Masson.

Giving Credit

6. A tramp stopped a gentleman in the street and asked him for the price of a night's lodging. The gentleman had no small change, but told the tramp he would be along there again in a few minutes, after he had made a

---

* Stories from *"The Best Stories in the World"* by Masson are used through the courtesy of Doubleday, Doran and Company.

few purchases, and would have some small change.

"Very good of you, indeed," remarked the tramp; "but sir, you have no idea how much money I lose by giving credit."

—*"The Best Stories in the World."*
Masson.

Nearly Every Night

7. A very prominent man recently died and shortly after a friend of the family called to condole with the widow. The caller had been a very warm friend of the man who had died, and as he was about to leave he asked:

"Did Will leave you very much?"

"Oh, yes, indeed," replied the widow, "nearly every night."

—*"The Best Stories in the World."*
Masson.

His Trial

8. A man, arrested for murder, bribed one of the men on the jury to hang out for a verdict of manslaughter. The jury were out a long time, and finally came in with a verdict of manslaughter.

The prisoner rushed up to the juror and said: "I'm obliged to you, my friend. Did you have a hard time?"

"Yes," said the man; "an awful hard time. The other eleven wanted to acquit you."

—"The Best Stories in the World."
Masson.

Limited

9. A small boy of a thoughtful turn of mind, sitting at his mother's feet one day, looked up and said suddenly:

"Mother, do liars go to heaven?"

"Why, no, dear," replied the mother in some surprise. "Certainly not."

There was quite a pause. Finally, the boy said quietly:

"Well, it must be mighty lonesome up there with only God and George Washington."

—"The Best Stories in the World."
Masson.

Patient Tommy

10. A visitor from the Sunday School said to Tommy:

"Why not come to our Sunday School? Several of your little friends have joined us lately."

Tommy thought for a moment and then said:

"Does a red-headed kid by the name of Jimmy Brown go to your Sunday School?"

"Yes, indeed," replied the new teacher.

"Well, then," said Tommy, with an air of interest, "I'll be there next Sunday, you bet. I've been layin' for that kid for three weeks, and never knew where to find him."

—*"The Best Stories in the World."*
Masson.

A Change in the Prescription

11. A miser who hated to part with money had been ill for a long time. To the doctor who was just bringing him around, he said one day:

"Ah, Doctor, we have known each other such a long time, I don't intend to insult you by settling your account in cash; but I have put you down for a handsome legacy in my will."

The doctor looked thoughtful. "Allow me,"

he said, "to look at that prescription again. I wish to make a slight alteration in it."

—*"The Best Stories in the World."*
Masson.

No Excuse

12. An office boy complained to the president of the company that he couldn't keep the visitors from going up to see him.

"When I say you are out they don't believe me. They say they must see you."

"Well, just tell them that's what they all say. I must have quiet somehow."

That afternoon a lady called at the office to see the president, and the boy told her it was impossible.

"But I must see him," she protested. "I'm his wife."

"That's what they all say," replied the boy.

—*"The Best Stories in the World."*
Masson.

Self Expression

13. Not very long ago a man in Boston noticed a little newsboy who was selling papers at the same place each morning. He was a little bit of a fellow, but he had a big voice. One day the gentleman stopped to ask him some questions.

"Where do you get your papers, son?" asked the gentleman.

"Oh, I buy them in the alley," said the small boy.

"And what do you pay for them?"

"Two cents."

"What do you sell them for?"

"Two cents."

"Then you don't make anything at all!"

"No, Sir," replied the boy, "but it gives me a chance to holler!"

At Ellis Island

14. One of the big ships had just come into the harbor. A long line of men and women were waiting for inspection, before landing.

There were men and women in that line from many foreign countries. An officer was talking to one of the men who was a Swede. The officer said, "What is your name?"

"Tom Olsen," answered the Swede.

"Are you married?" was the next question.

"Yes, I'm married," said the Swede, "but my wife is not here."

"Whom did you marry?" asked the officer.

"I married a woman."

The officer frowned. "Of course you did. Did you ever hear of anyone who didn't marry a woman?"

"Oh, yes," said the Swede with a smile. "My sister, she married a man!"

Suspension Bridges

15. Several traveling salesmen in the smoking car had been boasting of their sales. The figures ran up into the thousands and millions. One man sat by the window and said nothing. One of the others spoke to him and said:

"Well, brother, how about you? Has business been good?"

"Pretty good."

"Have you made any sales lately?"

"Well, I made one about six months ago."

"Is that so. When do you expect to make another?"

"Oh, in about a year and a half."

"What, one sale six months ago, and the next one in about a year and a half! Is your house satisfied with that record?"

"Seems to be," said the man.
"What do you sell, anyway?"
"Suspension bridges," was the reply.
—*"Make 'Em Laugh Again"—by Lurie.*

A Lesson in Physiology

16. A teacher was explaining to her class what an organ of the body is. She told them that an organ of the body is a part of the body set apart for some special use. For example, the eye is the organ of sight, the ear of hearing, etc.

After she had gone over the work pretty thoroughly, she wanted to find out how much her pupils knew of the subject. So she asked them who could tell what an organ of the body really is.

For some time there was no reply. Then the smallest boy in the room held up his hand. "I know," he said. "I see with my eye-organ, I hear with my ear-organ, I smell with my nose-organ, I eat with my mouth-organ, and I feel with my hand-organ."

An Eccentric Great Man

17. The handwriting of Horace Greeley was very illegible. Very few people could read what he wrote, and sometimes it puzzled Mr. Greeley himself.

He wrote a hurried note one day and addressed it to the editor of one of the other New York papers. A messenger boy was called and the note sent. The boy delivered it, but the man couldn't make it out and sent it back.

When the boy handed his own note to Mr. Greeley, he opened it and looked it over very carefully, supposing that it was a reply to his own communication. He was unable to read it and looking at the boy indignantly, said, "Why what does the old idiot mean?" "Yes," said the boy, "that's just what the other man said!"

First Class

18. A company of tourists were traveling in Switzerland. One day they were to take a coach trip up a mountain. Each one bought his own ticket for the journey. The American bought a first class ticket, but he noticed that all the others bought second or third class tickets.

When they all got into the same coach, the American said to the driver, "What advantage is there in paying for a first class ticket? The holders of the second and third class tickets have precisely the same accommodations."

The driver said, "You just wait and see."

So by and by they came to a steep hill and the driver called out, "First class passengers will keep their seats; second class passengers will get out and walk; third class passengers will get out and push."

A Vocal Standard

19. A well-known Doctor of Divinity was once touring a sparsely settled part of the country, and one night put up at a comfortable looking farm house, where he soon got upon friendly terms with the family. Next morning, coming down to breakfast, he found all the men folks had gone to work and the farmer's wife waiting to prepare his breakfast.

"How do you like your eggs?" she inquired.

"Medium well done," was the answer.

Whereupon the hostess retired to the kitchen whence in a few moments came the sound of her voice singing "Nearer My God to Thee." The doctor, being a good singer himself, joined heartily in this morning hymn.

After singing three verses the lady stopped and appeared with the eggs.

"Why didn't you sing the fourth verse?" the minister asked with a smile.

"Oh, you said you liked your eggs medium, so I sang three verses. It takes four verses to boil them hard."

The Bone of Contention

20. Booker T. Washington was fond of telling the story of an old colored man named Uncle Sam. He knew Uncle Sam in his boyhood days at Hale's Ford in Virginia.

Uncle Sam was very much interested in the Civil War, but he did not take any part in it. Each day he would go to his white friends for news of what was going on.

One day one of his white friends asked him why it was that he did not take part in the war. He reminded Uncle Sam that the men of the North and the men of the South were killing each other off because of him and his people. The white man said to him: "Why don't you pitch in and join them?"

Uncle Sam replied: "My friend, have you ever seen two dogs fighting over a bone?"

"Of course I have," said the white man.

"Did you ever see the bone fight?" said Uncle Sam.

Not Far To Go

21. A distinguished lawyer and politician was traveling on the train when an Irish woman came into the car with a big basket and bundle and sat down near him.

When the conductor came around to collect fares, the woman paid her money, and the conductor passed by the lawyer without collecting anything. The good woman thereupon said to the lawyer:

"Why is it that the conductor takes the money of a poor Irish woman and don't ask you, who seem to be a rich man, for anything?"

"My dear madam," replied the lawyer, who had a pass, "I am traveling on my beauty."

For a moment the woman looked at him, and then quickly answered:

"And is that so? Then you must be very near your journey's end."

Good Advice

22. There were two ladies riding in a car. One wished to have the window shut, as she said she took cold very easily and was afraid of drafts. The other wished to have the window open, for she liked fresh air and must have it. Neither lady was willing to give in. Finally, the conductor came to them.

"Conductor," said the first lady, "if this window remains open I may get a cold. It will kill me."

"Conductor," said the second lady, "if you shut this window I may suffocate."

The conductor did not know what to do. A man who was sitting in the corner said to the conductor:

"Open the window, my dear friend. That will kill one. Then shut it. That will kill the other. Then we can have peace."

Johnny Told the Truth

23. The pupils in a country school had been studying about the different seasons of the year. The teacher had explained to them very carefully what characteristics they would find in summer, autumn, winter and spring. She then asked some questions to make sure the pupils understood what she had been telling them.

After several questions had been asked and

answered, the teacher came to Johnny. He was a stupid boy who sat in the corner and never paid attention to anything.

"Well, Johnny," the teacher said, "have you been paying attention?"

"Yes'm," he answered promptly.

"I'm glad to hear it. Now can you tell me what there is in the spring?"

"Yes'm, I can, but I don't want to."

"Oh, yes you do. You have heard the other pupils answer. Be a good boy and don't be afraid. Now tell us what is in the spring."

Johnny stammered, "Why, why, mum, there's a frog, and a lizard, and a dead cat in it, but I didn't put 'em there. It was another boy. I saw him do it."

The Humbug

24. Charles Darwin had many friends among the English boys. He was especially fond of two boys who liked to play jokes on him.

One day these boys went out into the field and caught a butterfly, a grasshopper, a beetle and a centipede. Then they took the insects home to see what they could make out of them.

They used the body of the centipede, the wings of the butterfly, the legs of the grasshopper, and the head of the beetle. When they had glued all these together they made the strangest looking insect you ever saw.

The boys put their strange looking insect into a box and very carefully took it to Mr. Darwin to see if they could fool him.

"We caught this insect in a field," they said. "Can you tell us what it is, sir?"

Darwin looked at the insect. Then he looked at the boys. He smiled slightly, and asked:

"Did it hum when you caught it?"

"Yes, sir," they answered, nudging each other.

"Then," said Darwin, "it is a humbug."

The Pickpocket

25. It was late in the afternoon and the subway platform was crowded with people anxious to get home as quickly as possible.

When the train pulled into the station the crowd surged forward, carrying everyone with it. A small man was swept along with the crowd until he found himself wedged in the middle of the car with a very fat man and a very tall one.

As the train pulled out, the small man thought about pickpockets, and remembered that he had some money in his overcoat pocket. He put his hand into what he thought was his pocket to see if his money was safe. He found the hand of the fat man there. Grabbing the fat man's hand he glared at him and fairly shouted:

"You are a pickpocket, but I caught you that time."

The fat man glared back and roared: "Let go of my hand, you little rascal."

"Pickpocket," shouted the little man.

"Scoundrel," roared the fat one.

Just then the tall man looked up from the paper he had been reading over the heads of the crowd, and drawled:

"I'd like to get off here if you fellows don't mind taking your hands out of my pockets."

Uncle Ned's Old Aunt

26. Down South there was an old colored man called Uncle Ned. He had worked for the same family for a great many years, ever since the Civil War, in fact. At last one day he went to his master and said:

"Master, I'd like to have a vacation."

"What, Uncle Ned," said his master, "you want a vacation? What do you want a vacation for?"

"Why," said Uncle Ned, "I want to go up to Virginia."

"What do you want to go up to Virginia for, Uncle Ned?"

"Well, I reckon I want to see my old aunt."

"Your old aunt! I didn't know you had an old aunt up in Virginia."

"Yes, sah."

"And how old is she?"

"Well, I reckon she is one hundred and ten years old."

"One hundred and ten years old! You have an aunt up in Virginia as old as that?"

"Yes, sah."

"And what is your old aunt doing up in Virginia?"

"Why, I reckon she must be living with her grandmother."

Martha's View of Art

27. Chatsworth is the country home of the Duke of Devonshire. It is a beautiful old castle and contains many wonderful pictures.

When the Duke is not there the castle is thrown open to the public.

An old gentleman who lived near this famous residence, one day drove to Chatsworth with a party of friends. He took with him his housekeeper, Martha, a good old soul who had been with him for many years.

When the party arrived at Chatsworth they went slowly through room after room of almost priceless pictures. They noticed that Martha was not missing anything, although she did not say a word. She went up to each picture and examined it closely, much to the amusement of the rest of the party.

Finally her master turned to her and said:

"Well, Martha, what do you think of it all?"

"Why," exclaimed Martha, "I can't see a speck o' dust anywhere."

The Hare and the Tortoise

28. A hare one day made himself merry over the slow pace of the tortoise, and vainly boasted of his own great speed in running.

The tortoise took the laugh in good part. "Let us try a race," she said; "I will run with you five miles for five dollars, and the Fox out yonder shall be the judge."

The hare agreed and away they started together.

The tortoise never for a moment stopped, but jogged along with a slow, steady pace, straight to the end of the course. But the hare, full of sport, first outran the tortoise, then fell behind; having come midway to the goal, he began to nibble at the young herbage, and to amuse himself in many ways. After awhile, the day being warm, he lay down for a nap, saying, "If she should go by, I can easily enough catch up."

When he awoke, the tortoise was not in sight; and, running as fast as he could, he found her comfortably dozing at their goal, after her success was gained.

—From Stickney's edition of "Æsop's Fables," by courtesy of Messrs. Ginn and Company.

Willing to Repeat

29. The office boy to a large firm of publishers, when sent to one of the operative departments with a message, noticed that something was wrong with the machinery. He gave the alarm and thus prevented much damage. The circumstance was reported to the head of the firm before whom John was summoned.

"You have done me a great service, my boy," he said. "In future your wages will be increased $1 weekly."

"Thank you, sir," said the bright little fellow. "I'll do my best to be worth it, and to be a good servant to you."

The reply struck the chief almost as much as the lad's previous service had done.

"That's the right spirit," he said. "In all the years I have been in business no one has ever thanked me in that way. I will make the increase $2. Now, what do you say to that?"

"Well, sir," said the boy, after a moment's hesitation, "would you mind if I said it again?"

—*Philadelphia Public Ledger.*

Franklin's Toast

30. Benjamin Franklin was having dinner with two friends in London. One of the friends was an Englishman and the other a Frenchman. As three nationalities were represented, it was suggested that each of the men propose a toast to his own country.

The Englishman rose first, and in a proud and boastful manner, like a true John Bull, said:

"Here is to England, the sun that gives light to all the nations of the earth."

The Frenchman responded in the same proud and boastful manner, and said:

"Here is to France, the moon whose magic rays move the tides of the world."

Then Franklin rose, and assuming an air of quaint modesty, remarked:

"Here is to George Washington, the Joshua of America, who commanded the sun and the moon to stand still, and they stood still."

Please Call Her

31. A dignified, middle-aged gentleman was trying to read in a crowded train. Among the passengers in the car was a lady with a very sprightly little blue-eyed girl with golden hair and an inquisitive tongue, who made friends with everyone around her. She asked the dignified gentleman numerous questions, played with his watch chain, and endeavored to determine by means of the buttons on his waistcoat whether he was rich man, poor man, beggar man, or thief.

The mother fairly beamed upon him, as she was the type of woman who cannot understand that anyone might be annoyed by *her* child. However, the gentleman was becoming nervous, and rather tired of the interruptions, and turning to the lady, said:

"Madam, what do you call this sweet little child?"

"Ethel," replied the mother with a smile and evident pride.

"Please call her, then," said the gentleman as he resumed his reading.

Guess Who Sent Them

32. George and Ethel had been married only a short time. They had had a large wedding, and had received a great many handsome presents, including the usual silverware and jewelry. Because of the prominence of the bride's family, the newspapers had commented on the number and value of the many gifts.

When they returned from their honeymoon

they went to live in a pretty little cottage in the suburbs. A few days after they had settled in their new home they received in the mail one morning two tickets for the evening performance at a city theatre, together with a note which read: "Guess who sent them?" They found it impossible to identify the handwriting or to guess the donor, but nevertheless they decided to use them and have a good time.

When they reached home after a very enjoyable evening, and switched on the lights, they found the place stripped of jewelry and silverware. But on the dining room table was another note in the same handwriting which read: "Now you know!"

An Absent-Minded Philosopher

33. One evening Sir Isaac Newton went into his room where a fire had just been lighted in the grate. It was an unusually cold day in the middle of winter, and he put his chair as close to the grate as he could so that he could get all the warmth there was.

By degrees the fire burned up and he became intolerably hot. He rang his bell violently for John, his man servant. John did not come for sometime. When he did appear Sir Isaac was almost roasted.

He spoke to John in an irritable tone that was very unusual for such an amiable and placid philosopher.

"Remove the grate, you lazy rascal. Remove the grate before I am burned to death."

John, who knew his master's ways, said a little waggishly:

"Might you not rather draw back your chair?"

"Upon my word, I never thought of that," said Sir Isaac, smiling.

Puddin'head Wilson

34. The late President Wilson and Colonel George Harvey were close friends. Both men had brilliant minds and a keen sense of humor. Their friends said it was as good as a play to watch the flashes of wit that would spring from a crossing of those two keen minds.

One time when Colonel Harvey was lunching at the White House Mark Twain's name came up in some connection, and Colonel Harvey remarked that there are still living persons who have never heard of Mark Twain. The President found this hard to believe.

"Oh, yes," Colonel Harvey continued, "only yesterday in Washington I met such a one. He was an office seeker. He declared positively that he had never heard of Mark Twain. I asked him about Tom Sawyer, and he said, No, he'd never heard of him either. Nor Huckleberry Finn? No, never. Nor Puddin'head Wilson? 'Oh, Lord, yes,' he exclaimed, 'I voted for him.'"

When the President's roars of laughter had subsided, Colonel Harvey continued, "The office seeker added wistfully, 'That's all the good it done me.'"

A Sword Puzzle

35. When the first Napoleon was emperor of France he instituted the Cross of the Legion of Honor as a reward of merit for unusual bravery. Every soldier of France hoped to win this cross.

One day Napoleon met an old soldier and stopped to talk with him. He saw at once that the old man had lost one arm, and he asked him where he had lost his arm.

"At the battle of Austerlitz, your Majesty," replied the old soldier. He told Napoleon of the brave deed that had left him with but one arm.

"Were you not decorated for this?" asked Napoleon.

"No, your Majesty," replied the old man.

"Then here is my cross for you. I make you chevalier." And Napoleon took the cross he was wearing and pinned it on the coat of the old soldier.

The old soldier was surprised and delighted, and said:

"Your Majesty makes me chevalier because I have lost one arm. What would your Majesty do if I had lost both arms?"

"Oh, in that case I should make you an officer of the Legion."

Whereupon the soldier immediately drew his sword and cut off his other arm.

There is no particular reason to doubt this story. The only question is, how did he do it?

The Fortunes of War

36. A woman of social prominence lived near one of the big training camps during the

World War. She liked to entertain the officers in her home, and always had one or more for dinner on Sunday. She was careful never to include a private among her guests. She took an especial fancy to a young Lieutenant, and had him for dinner more often than any of the other men.

One Sunday, when she was expecting this young officer for dinner, he found at the last minute that he could not get off duty. He asked a private to go in his place, and he gave him a note to his hostess explaining why he could not get away, and saying that he was sending a friend in his place.

When the private presented the note to his hostess, she showed very plainly that she was not pleased with the substitute. The atmosphere was so uncomfortable that he had the good sense not to remain for dinner.

The next time the Lieutenant had dinner with this lady she told him she did not like the substitute he had sent. "Why did you send me a private?" she demanded. "I wanted an officer."

The Lieutenant replied, much to the chagrin of his hostess: "I am sorry you did not like my friend. He is a fine fellow. Before the war I was his chauffeur."

Hope Deferred

37. They sat each at an extreme end of the horse-hair sofa. They had been courting now for something like two years, but the wide gap between had always been respectfully preserved.

"A penny for your thoughts, Sandy," murmured Maggie, after a silence of an hour and a half.

"Well," replied Sandy slowly, with surprising boldness, "to tell you the truth, I was just thinking how fine it would be if you were to give me a bit of a kiss."

"I've no objection," simpered Maggie, moving over; and she kissed him plumply on the tip of his left ear.

Sandy relapsed into a brown study once more, and the clock ticked twenty-seven minutes.

"And what are you thinking about now—another, eh?"

"No, no; it's more serious now."

"Is it?" asked Maggie softly. Her heart

was going pit-a-pat with expectation. "And what might it be?"

"I was just thinking," answered Sandy, "that it was about time you were paying me that penny."

Father Won't Like It

38. It was noon time of a very warm day in August. A man walking home to dinner saw a small boy doing his best to pile a load of hay back on the cart from which it had fallen. The sun was beating down on the uncovered head of the poor little fellow, and his face was red from the heat and exertion.

"You can't get that hay on there alone," said the man. "Come home to dinner with me, and afterwards I will help you."

"Thank you," said the boy, "but I can't do it. My father won't like it."

"Oh, come along," said the man. "You can work much better after you have had something to eat."

"No," said the boy very firmly. "My father will be angry if I do."

"I know that your father wouldn't want you to work in this heat on an empty stomach. Come along and have a good meal."

So the boy went very reluctantly, and all through the meal and after he was saying that he knew his father wouldn't like it. Finally, the man said: "Well, where is your father?" And the boy replied, "He is under the load of hay."

Dust on the Atlantic

39. When Mr. Knox was Secretary of State he had a colored messenger in his office named William. William knew something about geography and was always trying to show off.

A globe of the world about six feet high stood beside Mr. Knox's desk. One day when he turned to it to decide some important question, he found that dust on the globe had soiled his coat sleeve. Mr. Knox was a very particular man, and was somewhat irritated to find the dust on his sleeve.

He spoke sharply to William, and laying his finger on the globe, he said:

"The dust there is a foot thick."

"It's thicker than that, Mr. Secretary," replied the Negro with the familiarity that comes of mingling with greatness.

"What do you mean?" demanded Mr. Knox.

"Why, you'se got your finger on the Desert of Sahara."

Mr. Knox tried hard not to smile.

"You'll find some on the Atlantic Ocean, too," he remarked as he turned to his desk.

Mark Twain and Whistler

40. A friend tells an amusing story about the first meeting between Mark Twain, the humorist, and James McNeill Whistler, the artist.

The friend warned Mark Twain that Whistler was a confirmed joker, and Twain had replied that he would get the better of Whistler should the latter attempt any "funny business." Furthermore, he was determined to anticipate Whistler if possible.

The two men were introduced in Whistler's studio, and Mark Twain assumed an air of hopeless stupidity. He went up to a painting that had just been completed and said:

"Not at all bad, Mr. Whistler, not at all bad; only, if I were you, I would do away with that cloud," and he made a motion as if to do away with a cloud effect.

Mr. Whistler was almost beside himself. "Great heavens, sir!" he exclaimed, "do be careful not to touch that; the paint is not yet dry."

"Oh, I don't mind that," replied Mark Twain with an air of perfect nonchalance, "you see I am wearing old gloves."

Mr. Choate Was Obliging

41. When Mr. Choate was our ambassador to the Court of St. James's, he was one evening attending a function at which many other diplomats were present. They, of course, wore full regimentals, while Mr. Choate wore the simple evening dress of the American gentleman. Some of the men servants also wore evening dress, a custom that has its embarrassments.

At a late hour Mr. Choate was standing by the door when a foreign diplomat approached him, and mistaking him for a servant, said to him:

"Call me a cab."

"You are a cab, sir," readily responded Mr. Choate.

The diplomat was very indignant and complained to his host that one of the servants had insulted him. He pointed out the man by the door.

"Why, that is not a servant; that is Ambassador Choate," said his host. "Come over and I will introduce you."

The diplomat was very much chagrined, and he made his apologies to the American ambassador.

"Oh, that's all right," said Mr. Choate. "But if you had only been better looking, I'd have called you a hansom cab."

A Touching Message

42. The following story is told of Mr. George Broadhurst, the playwright, who is an Englishman. He had been staying for a week at one of the large hotels in London, and left at a late hour at night. When he left his room he was surprised to see an endless procession of waiters, maids, porters and pages come forward with the expectant smile and empty hand. When each one had been generously tipped, Mr. Broadhurst dashed for the cab at the door.

Just as he was settling himself with a sigh of relief, a page popped his head into the window and breathlessly exclaimed:

"I beg pardon, sir, but the night-lift man says he's waiting for a message from you, sir."

"The night-lift man wants a message from me?"

"Yes, sir; he says he can't go to sleep without a message from you, sir."

"Really, he can't go to sleep without a message from me?"

"No, sir."

"How touching. Then tell him, 'Pleasant dreams.'"

It Worked Out to a Cent

43. The visitor was an Englishman. He was paying his first visit to America, having come to see his married daughter and his new grandson.

The steamer landed earlier than was expected and there was no one at the dock to greet him. But he knew his daughter's address —it was only six blocks across town from the wharves—and in a short time a taxicab landed him at the proper destination. His daughter was very much surprised to see him.

"But, father," she asked, after he had been welcomed, "did you have any difficulty getting here?"

"Not at all," he said. "The only thing that perplexed me was your Yankee money. On the ship I had two pounds changed into American coins. The purser tried to explain their value, but I couldn't understand him.

"Well, then, how did you pay your taxi fare?"

"When the cab stopped in front of the house," he said, "I just fished out of my pocket all the Yankee money the purser had given me—quite a handful of it, I assure you—and I held it out to the cab driver, so that he might take his fare!"

"How much did he take?"

"That's the extraordinary part of it," said the Britisher; "he took it all. By a remarkable coincidence I had produced the exact amount due."

Ready for the Summer Boarder

44. The dignified president of a well-known and flourishing New England college tells the following story at his own expense:

One summer some years ago he spent a vacation of several weeks at a farmhouse in a Maine town. The next season he received a letter from his former boarding mistress inquiring if he would like to return.

In reply he stated that he would be very

glad to pass another summer vacation with her, provided some needed changes were made about the place.

"First," wrote the college president, "your maid Mary is anything but neat and orderly in her ways, and if she is still with you I trust you will at least not allow her to wait on the table.

"Secondly, I would suggest that the sanitary conditions on your place would be greatly improved if the pigsty were moved back a few rods further from the house or done away with altogether.

"I will wait until I hear from you before deciding about coming."

The somewhat particular college president was reassured by the receipt of the following reply:

"Mary has went. We ain't had no hogs on the place since you was here last summer. Be sure and come."

Billy Bulger's Half

45. Billy Bulger was a dilapidated old man who went around asking for work, knowing very well that no work would be entrusted to him. When work was refused, he always asked for a contribution, and usually received it.

One morning he greeted Mr. Boyd with the usual, "Got any work for me this morning, Mistah Boyd?"

"No," was the response, and before Billy could ask for the contribution, he added:

"But wait a minute. Lawyer Phillips has owed me twenty dollars for twenty years. Collect it and I'll give you half."

Old Billy shuffled out in search of Lawyer Phillips. He found him in the middle of a group of clients and influential citizens. Elbowing his way through the group, he called out in a loud voice:

"Mistah Phillips, suh!"

"Well?" asked the lawyer, much annoyed.

"Mistah Boyd done tell me that you've owed him twenty dollars for about a hundred years. He wants to know can you pay him, suh."

The lawyer hurried to Billy's side.

"You idiot," he said, "Do you want to ruin my business? Here!" and he put a ten dollar bill into the old man's hand.

Billy went straight back to Mr. Boyd, who said:

"Well, Billy, did you get it?"

"I got my half all right, but you'd better look out when you go back to get your half—he's right smart hot over it, suh!"

Why the Stove Was Elevated

46. Two college professors were one time the guests of a college chum at a hunting camp in the woods. When they entered the camp their attention was attracted to the unusual position of the stove, which was set on posts about four feet high.

One of the professors began to comment on the knowledge woodsmen gain by observation. "Now," said he, "this man discovered that the heat radiating from the stove strikes the roof, and the circulation is so quickened that the camp is warmed in much less time than would be required if the stove were in its regular place on the floor."

The other professor was of the opinion that the stove was elevated to be above the window in order that cool and pure air could be had at night.

The host, being more practical, contended that the stove was elevated in order that a good supply of green wood could be placed beneath it to dry.

After considerable argument each man placed a dollar bill upon the table, and it was agreed that the one whose opinion was nearest the guide's reason for elevating the stove should take the pool.

The guide was called and asked why the stove was placed in such an unusual position.

"Well," said he, "when I brought the stove up the river I lost most of the stove pipe overboard, and I had to set the stove up there so as to have the pipe reach the roof."

He got the money.

—*Boston Herald.*

Miser Brown

47. John Wanamaker was reproving some of his Sunday School pupils for laughing at a deaf boy's wrong answers to misunderstood questions, and he said:

"Boys, it isn't right to laugh at anyone's affliction. Besides, you never know when your own words may be turned against you. I once knew a deaf man—let us call him Brown—who was disposed to stinginess. He never married; but he was very fond of society, so one day he felt compelled to give a banquet to the many ladies and gentlemen whose guest he had been.

"They were amazed that his purse-strings had been unloosed so far, and they thought he deserved encouragement, so it was arranged that he should be toasted. One of the most daring young men of the company was selected; for it took a lot of nerve to frame and propose a toast to so unpopular a man as Miser Brown. But the young man rose. And this is what was heard by everyone except Brown, who never heard anything that was not roared into his ear:

"'Here's to you, Miser Brown. You are no better than a tramp, and it is suspected that you got most of your money dishonestly. We trust that you may get your just deserts yet, and land in the penitentiary.'

"Visible evidences of applause made Brown smile with gratification. He got to his feet, raised his glass to his lips, and said: 'The same to you, sir.'"

—*Marshall P. Wilder, in the New York Tribune.*

Why He Was a Democrat

48. "We had an interesting old teacher in the small country school near my home of

Peekskill," said Senator Depew. "He had drilled a number of his brightest pupils in the history of politics. To test them, he called upon three and demanded a declaration of personal political principles.

"You are a Republican, Tom, are you not?" inquired the teacher of the first. "Yes, sir," was the answer. "And Bill, you are a prohibitionist, I believe?" "Yes, sir," said Bill. "And Jim, you are a Democrat?" "Yes, sir," said Jim.

"Well, now," continued the teacher, "I want each one of you to give me a good reason why you belong to your particular party. To the one who gives the best reason, I will give this woodchuck that I caught on the way to school this morning."

"I am a Republican," said Tom, "because the Republican party saved the country in the war and abolished slavery."

"And I am a prohibitionist," said Bill, remembering his careful instruction, "because rum is our country's greatest enemy. It is the cause of our overcrowded prisons and poorhouses."

"Very excellent reasons, boys, very excellent reasons," observed the teacher encouragingly.

"And, now, Jim, why are you a Democrat?"

"Well, sir," was the slow reply, "I am a Democrat because I want that woodchuck."

A Good Investment

49. Now, James, said a business man to his ten-year-old boy, you are going to be a business man some day and I think you should have a few lessons in the art of investing money. Here is half a dollar. Take it and go downtown. Look around carefully and invest it to the best advantage. Be sure to put it where it will be safe and bring you a good interest.

The boy took the silver and started off. In an hour he returned, reporting that he had made a good investment. He said that he was going to get one hundred per cent interest.

His father was amazed. "One hundred per cent! Splendid! How did you invest it?"

"Well," said the boy, "I went downtown and walked around and finally came to a church. There was a meeting and they were singing, so I went in. It was a missionary meeting and a man was asking for money for missions. He said that if you gave your money to the Lord he would send it back to you doubled—He would pay you a hundred per cent interest. So

I put that half dollar in the collection plate."

The father was disgusted with the business ability of his small son. "Why, my boy, you will never see that half dollar again. You will never make a business man if you believe everything you hear!"

The boy looked so downcast and discouraged that his father laughingly gave him a silver dollar, saying, "Well, son, you have made a bad mistake, but I am going to give you one more chance. Take this dollar and invest it, and be sure you stay away from missionary meetings!"

"Why, father!" exclaimed the boy as he took the dollar, "that man was right after all. The Lord did send back my half dollar, and with one hundred per cent interest, too!"

Efficiency

50. The owner of a large factory hired an efficiency expert to reorganize the business.

The first morning the expert had walked through only one department when he saw a lazy-looking man in overalls sitting on a bench and doing nothing but chew tobacco.

The expert watched the man for a few minutes, and became very much out of patience as he did so.

He walked over to the man and said, "See here, what do you think you are doing?"

"Nothin'," said the man.

"Well, what have you been doing?" asked the expert.

"Nothin'," was the reply.

"And how long have you been sitting there doing nothing?" asked the expert.

"Oh, about an hour—maybe an hour and a half," was the answer.

"Is that so. And how much money do you get a week?" inquired the expert.

"Twenty-four dollars a week," said the man.

"Well," said the expert, "we will stop that part of it right now. When is your week up?"

"Tomorrow," said the man.

"You needn't wait until tomorrow. You are fired now," said the expert as he reached into his pocket and took four five dollar bills and four ones from his own roll. He handed the money to the man and said, "Get out of here, and don't ever let me see you again inside this factory."

The man slouched out, and the expert said to himself, "There is nothing like starting reform at once." Then he called the foreman of the department and asked, "Who is that fellow walking out of the door?"

"I don't know his name," said the foreman, "but he has a job in the foundry across the street."

LESSONS ON THE MOVEMENTS

Lip-reading is based on the movements that represent the sounds (not letters) of the consonants, vowels and diphthongs. Some movements are plainly seen and easily learned, as the Lips-Shut Movement for the sounds of p, b and m, while others are so obscure as to require the help of the context for their recognition, as the Throat Movement for the sounds of k, hard c, hard g, ng, and nk.

The consonants are divided into four groups, as follows:

1. Those formed and revealed by the lips.
    (a) P, b, m, mp and mb—Lips-Shut.
    (b) F and v,—ph and gh—Lip-to-Teeth.
    (c) Wh and w—Puckered-Variable.
2. Those formed by the tongue and revealed by the lips.
    (a) R—Puckered Corners.
    (b) S, z and soft c—Extended-Narrow.

(c) Sh, zh, ch, j, soft g—Lips-Projected.

3. Those formed and revealed by the tongue.
   (a) Th—Tongue-to-Teeth.
   (b) L—Pointed-tongue-to-Gum.
   (c) T, d, n, nt, nd—Flat-Tongue-to-Gum.

4. Those revealed by the context.
   (a) Y—Relaxed-Narrow.
   (b) K, hard c, hard g, ng and nk—Throat-Movement.
   (c) H—No Movement (Aspirate).

The vowels fall into three groups, i. e., puckered, relaxed and extended, and each group has three widths of opening between the lips, narrow, medium and wide. The diagram below will make this clear.

Width of Opening	Shape of lips		
	Puckered	Relaxed	Extended
Narrow	Long o͞o (coon)	Short ĭ (kid)	Long ē (keen)
Medium	Short o͝o (good)	Short ŭ (cut)	Short ĕ (get)
Wide	Aw (caw)	Ah (cart)	Short ă (cat)

LESSONS ON MOVEMENTS

There are two groups of diphthongs, i. e.

1. Those with a puckered final movement.
   (a) Ow, as in "how." Relaxed-Wide, followed by a puckered movement.
   (b) Long ō, as in "go." Contracting puckered movement.
   (c) Long ū, as in "mute." Relaxed-Narrow and Puckered-Narrow.
2. Those with relaxed and narrow final movement.
   (a) Long ī, as in "pipe." Relaxed-Wide and Relaxed-Narrow.
   (b) Long ā, as in "late." Extended-Medium and Relaxed-Narrow.
   (c) Oy, as in "boy." Puckered-Wide and Relaxed-Narrow.

In developing the Lessons on the Movements the aim has been to group the consonants and vowel sounds so that the maximum of value can be gained from contrast and review.

As the Lips-Shut Movement for the sounds of p, b and m is the most easily recognized, it was chosen for the first lesson. Because the Extended-Narrow Movement for the sound of long ē is more nearly like the Lips-Shut Movement than any of the other vowels, it was combined with the sounds of p, b and m in the Movement Words, and is studied in the second lesson.

The principle adhered to throughout the book in developing *Movement Words* is to introduce only one new visible movement in combination with all movements previously studied, so far as possible. For this reason the same group of Movement Words is used in the second lesson as in the first, the attention being centered on the movement for long ē in the second lesson.

As each group of vowel sounds has three widths of opening—narrow, medium and wide —and long ē, Extended-Narrow, was studied in the second lesson, naturally the lesson to follow is based on the Extended-Medium Movement for short ĕ, and the fourth lesson on the Extended-Wide Movement for short ă, thus giving drill on the three extended movements in combination with p, b and m. The fifth and sixth lessons on F and v, Lip-to-Teeth, and Wh and w, Puckered-Variable, respectively, complete one group of three consonants and one of three vowels. This order is followed thereafter.

A glance at the Movement Words will show

the value of the development. For the first four lessons, p, b and m are combined with, first, long ē, (lessons one and two). Second with long ē and short ĕ, (lesson three), and third with long ē, and short ĕ and short ă, (lesson four). The obscure sounds of t, d and n; h, or k, g, ng, nk may be used for the purpose of making words. This development of the Movement Words provides the student with constant repetition and review of all the movements studied.

The *Contrast Words* are intended for contrast only, and the movements to be contrasted are combined with others that seem best for the purpose, regardless of whether or not they have been studied.

The *Practise Words* are in no sense a vocabulary to be learned, but are words grouped together to give the maximum number of combinations with and variations of the movement being studied, and are intended to be used to train the eyes and the mind along certain definite lines that are essential to quick lip-reading.

When the lesson for the day is on a consonant movement, that particular movement is combined in the Practise Words with all of the vowels in the order in which they are studied, with the consonant movement both before and after the vowels. If the lesson is on a vowel movement, then it is combined with all of the consonants in a similar way.

It is not intended that the student shall *learn* all of these movements, but it is intended that he shall *develop associations which translate movements into words.*

Lessons on double consonants have been introduced to provide the drill on double consonants for which so many teachers have asked, and also to give variety to the lessons. The Movement Words are an adaptation of the double consonant exercises in the original textbook. Placed as they are, these lessons do not interfere with the original sequence of lessons on the movements and may or may not be used in the order in which they appear, as seems best. The Practise Words and Sentences have been developed to conform to the other lessons on the movements.

The method of learning the movements involves, first, a clear conception of their characteristics, and, second, much practise in the observation of them. The aim of the practise is to make the recognition of the sound movements an unconscious act; that is, by much repetition to make the association of certain movements with certain sounds a habit, something which we do without the consciousness of effort or concentration.

It is analogous to the way in which we read the printed page. We do not think of each letter, nor even of each word, but rather of the thought conveyed. Just as we have made our knowledge and recognition of the printed letters a matter of habit, performed unconsciously, so should we endeavor to make our recognition of the sound movements an unconscious process.

Perfection in this ability to see the sounds is impossible, and for two reasons. First, because no two mouths are the same, and, second, because some of the movements are so slight and quick that the eye, while it may see them sometimes, cannot be sure of always seeing them.

The way to practise for these difficult sounds is not by an exaggeration of their movements. It is a waste of time to try to make the eye see by "mouthing" what cannot be seen in ordinary conversation. The aim should be to know these difficult sounds as well as possible when they appear in words, but not to waste energy in striving for an impossible perfection. Also, the aim should be to know the easier movements with an almost infallible accuracy, leaving to the mind the task of supplying the difficult ones from the thought of the sentence.

The only true way of studying the sounds is by observing the formations as they occur in words, and not singly by themselves. Thus if the student wishes to study the formation of long $\bar{oo}$ he should take a word containing it, as *moon,* and concentrate his attention on the long $\bar{oo}$ as he sees the whole word.

This is the only way of seeing the formations as movements, formed naturally and without exaggeration, and it is the only way to avoid mispronunciation. Almost any sound *tends* to be mouthed, or exaggerated, when pronounced alone, and some sounds, such as *w* and *r* cannot be correctly pronounced alone except by an expert.

To practise words simply for the sake of the word, that is, to try to memorize them as one would a vocabulary, is the least helpful form of word-study. The analogy between the study of lip-reading and the study of a foreign language does not hold here. Certainly some good can be obtained from such practise, *but it is not possible so to memorize word forma-*

tions that the eye will infallibly recognize them whenever seen.

There are several ways to practise words. They may be used to train the eyes in accuracy of observation of the sound formations, to train the mind in quickness of associated thought, and to train both eye and mind in alertness of response.

Mirror practise is the best way to train the eyes in accuracy of observation of the sound formations, and the method of mirror practise with the *Movement* and *Contrast Words* is best explained by taking the words of a lesson for illustration. The lesson on Ah-Relaxed-Wide is typical. The words are:

<pre>
bid bud bard—hip hup harp
fin fun far—give cuff carve
     bat bard—ham harm
     fat far—have carve
</pre>

In the first four groups the vowel sounds of short *ĭ* (relaxed-narrow), short *ŭ* (relaxed-medium), and *ah* (relaxed-wide), are combined with the consonants *p, b* and *m,* and *f* and *v,* both before and after the vowels. In the second four groups of words, the short *ă* (extended-wide), and *ah* (relaxed-wide), are combined with the same consonants in the same way.

When practising these words with the mirror take the first group of words—bid, bud, bard—and say them naturally and smoothly, to give the effect of natural speech, and watch in the mirror to see the different widths of opening for the vowel sounds. Then say the same group several times in different order, as "bard, bud, bid," "bud, bard, bid," "bid, bard, bud," each time watching for the different widths of opening for the three vowels. Then each of the groups of words should be practised in the same way.

After this has been done, take the words—bad, bard—and watch in the mirror to see the difference between the extended-wide movement for the short *ă* and the relaxed-wide movement for *ah*. Practise these words as directed above, and also the other three groups.

As has been said, mirror practise must be definite if it is to have value. It is so easy to let the mind wander, to make only vague associations, that we might just as well not practise with the mirror at all unless we can find a way to fix our attention definitely and in detail upon the thing we are looking for.

One of the values gained from mirror practise, that is often overlooked, is from *feeling* the formation of the sounds as they are repeated. When practising with the mirror be sure to use voice, and repeat the words a second time, thinking of the motor sensation of the words or movements as they are repeated.

The *Practise Words* should be practised with the mirror for all of the sounds in them, even though they have not been studied in the lessons. Do not lose sight of the fact that the Practise Words are *not* to be learned as a vocabulary. They are words grouped together to give the maximum number of combinations with and variations of the movement being studied for the day.

The method of practising these words with the mirror is to say each word over as many times as there are sounds (not letters), and each time the word is repeated naturally and without exaggeration, to think of the movement for one sound. The first time the word is repeated, watch for the movement for the first sound; the second time, for the second sound, and so on. If the movement has been studied, think of the characteristics of that movement before saying the word and try to see them. If the sound-movement is one that has not been studied, then watch for it in the mirror and see if any movement can be detected.

In the word "bought," for instance, there are three sounds—b-aw-t. When studying this word with the mirror say the whole word three times. The first time try to see the lips-shut movement for the *b*. The second time, watch for the puckering of the *aw*, and the third time the word is repeated, watch the tongue for the *t*. Because the vowel sound of *aw* opens the lips rather wide the tongue may be seen as it leaves the upper gum just back of the teeth. If no movement can be seen for a sound when the word is repeated naturally, do not try to make it visible by exaggeration, but remember that it could not be seen in natural speech, and that it will be supplied by the context.

Only the characteristics of the movements that have been studied will be known to the student, but he should watch for each sound and see what he can see. *He must not try to memorize what he sees.* He should see it, and feel it, and keep ever before his mind the thought that the aim of the practise is to make the recognition of the sound-movements an unconscious act; that is, by much repetition to make the association of certain movements with certain sounds a habit, something which we do without the consciousness of effort or concentration. *Such habits of association can be formed only by repetition in practise;* when formed, the mind is left free to concentrate on the thought of the speaker, not on how he is forming his speech, but on what he is saying.

The student should try *not* to think of the movements or words when actually reading the lips, for the human mind naturally takes in the thought as a whole and not one word at a time. Just as it would be difficult to get much of the content of the printed page if we stopped to think of each letter or word, so it is difficult, when reading the lips, to understand the thought of the speaker if we try to see movements and words.

Another method of practising *Practise Words* at home is to have someone give original sentences based on each word of the group. The assistant should give the word and the student should repeat it if he can. If he cannot see the word after two or three trials it should be shown to him. Then the assistant should let him see it on his lips, and should then put it into a sentence, the student to understand the *thought* of the sentence. A sentence should be given for each one of the *Practise Words*. Take the word "bought," for instance. Sentences suggested by this word might be, "I have bought all of my Christmas presents," "I bought the groceries on my way home," "We have just bought a house in the country," etc.

The *Sentences* immediately following the Practise Words use the words in the group above, but are intended for mind training, except when used for mirror practise. They train the mind through thought-getting, association of ideas, quickness, visual memory (by not allowing interruption until the sentence is completed), and alertness because the thought changes with each sentence.

The student should have someone at home give these sentences to him. He will be familiar with them, having had them in the lesson, and so the work should be given as rapidly as possible. He should not watch for or repeat the special word around which the sentence is built. And he should not repeat the sentence, as that requires a word-by-word understanding, but he should respond by a nod of the head, or in some way indicate that he has understood the sentence. One sentence should follow another as quickly as the assistant gets a response, as the practise of going quickly from one thought to another in this way is splendid training for alertness in understanding conversation.

The method of mirror practise with the sentences is the same as that for the stories. See p. 35.

Consonants Formed and Revealed by the Lips

P, b, m—Lips-Shut

51. For *p,* as in "pie," *b,* as in "by," and *m,* as in "my," the *lips* open from a *shut* position. It is the same for each in *ordinary, rapid* speech; the sounds must be told one from the other by the context.

52. *Movement Words*

pea—heap
bee—ēeb
me—deem

53. *Practise Words*

pea	moon	lip	bough
met	book	up	mow
pan	bought	arms	same
pin	creep	loop	pipe
bud	gem	bird	boys
part	lamb		

54.   *Sentences*

1. The sweet *peas* are in full bloom. 2. Where have I *met* you before? 3. The potatoes were browned in the *pan*. 4. If you see a *pin* pick it up. 5. The roses have just begun to *bud*. 6. The best of friends must *part*. 7. There will be a full *moon* tonight. 8. What *book* are you reading? 9. I *bought* the book for two dollars and a half. 10. The baby has just begun to *creep*. 11. Our new maid is a perfect *gem*. 12. Would you like a *lamb* chop for lunch? 13. You must keep a stiff upper *lip*. 14. Will you go *up*stairs for me? 15. My *arms* are lame from swimming. 16. Will you *loop* the loop with me? 17. The *bird* built its nest in the tree in front of the house. 18. The *bough* of the tree was broken by the wind. 19. The farmer will *mow* the field today. 20. We are all in the *same* boat. 21. Do you smoke a *pipe*? 22. The *boys* are playing ball.

EXTENDED VOWELS

Long ē—Extended-Narrow

55. For the sound of long *ē,* as in "keen," the lips are slightly drawn back, or *extended,*

at the corners, and the opening between the lips is *narrow*.

56. *Movement Words*

pea—heap
bee—eeb
me—deem

57. *Practise Words*

b*ee*	ch*ea*p¹	k*ee*p	m*ea*l⁵
f*ee*	th*e*me	p*ie*ce	p*ee*l⁵
w*e*	l*ea*f²	p*ea*ch⁴	m*ee*t⁶
r*ea*p	l*ea*ve²	b*ea*ch⁴	b*ea*t⁶
s*ee*m	t*ea*m³	t*ee*th	p*ea*k
*sh*ee*p¹	d*ee*p³		

58. *Sentences*

1. The *bee* was buzzing around the hive. 2. What *fee* does the lawyer charge? 3. Shall *we* take a walk through the fields? 4. The farmer will *reap* his harvest in the fall. 5. You *seem* to be very well. 6. How many *sheep* are in the fold? 7. I do not like to buy *cheap* things. 8.

* Words marked with the same numbers look alike on the lip, or are homophenous, and must be told by the contex.

What is the *theme* of the story? 9. There was not a *leaf* on the tree. 10. We must *leave* for our trip early in the morning. 11. The water in the river is very *deep*. 12. How many men are on the football *team*? 13. You may *keep* the book for a week. 14. Will you have a *piece* of pie? 15. There are three *peach* trees on the place. 16. We walked up and down the *beach* for an hour. 17. How many *teeth* has the baby? 18. The boys cannot wait for the next *meal*. 19. Will you *peel* the apple for me? 20. Where shall I *meet* you? 21. You must *beat* the fudge until it thickens. 22. The mountain *peak* is always covered with snow.

Short ĕ—Extended-Medium

59. For the sound of short ĕ, as in "get," the lips are slightly extended at the corners, and the opening between the lips is neither narrow, nor wide, but is *medium*. The *a*, as in "care," has also this extended-medium movement.

60. *Movement Words*

peat p*e*t—h*e*ap h*e*p
b*e*et b*e*t—*ee*b *e*bb
m*ee*t m*e*t—t*ea*m h*e*m

61. *Contrast Words*

Notice that for short ĕ the lips are more open than for long ē.

    dell—deal   fed—feed
    bed—bead   red—reed
    said—seed   well—wheel

62. *Practise Words*

bell	shell	help	wet
fell	shelf	wedge	beg
well	them	breath	bare
rest	left	smell[1]	melt[2]
sell	tell	spell[1]	belt[2]
send	kept		

63. *Sentences*

1. Did you hear the door *bell* ring? 2. The bowl broke when it *fell* on the floor. 3. The water from the *well* is very cold. 4. You should *rest* your eyes when they are tired. 5. How much will you *sell* the house for? 6. You must *send* the telegram as soon as you arrive. 7. Will you *shell* the peas for me? 8. You will find the book on the *shelf*. 9. When did you

see *them* last? 10. Can you write with your *left* hand? 11. Will you please *tell* us about your trip abroad? 12. I am afraid I *kept* you waiting. 13. Will you *help* me with my work? 14. Don't try to *wedge* your way through the crowd. 15. There is hardly a *breath* of air in the room. 16. I *smell* the food cooking over the fire. 17. How do you *spell* your name? 18. The weather has been very *wet*. 19. I made the dog *beg* for his supper. 20. The pebbles on the beach hurt my *bare* feet. 21. This warm weather will soon *melt* the snow. 22. The dress has a red leather *belt*.

Short ă—Extended-Wide

64. For the sound of short ă, as in "cat," the lips are slightly *extended* at the corners, and the opening between the lips is the *widest* of the extended vowels.

65.   *Movement Words*

peat pet pat—heap, hep hap
beet bet bat—eeb ebb ab
meet met mat—team hem ham

66.   *Contrast Words*

Notice that the lips are more open for short ă than for short ĕ.

    lad—led   tan—ten
    sad—said   fan—fen
    bad—bed   shad—shed

67.   *Practise Words*

bad[1]	sham[3]	tap[5]	bag[6]
man[1]	jam[3]	cap	back[6]
fat[2]	that	ham	bank[6]
fan[2]	lamp[4]	have	map
rap	lap[4]	hash	stamp
sap	tab[5]	pal	

68.   *Sentences*

1. The country roads are *bad* in the spring. 2. I watched a *man* climb to the top of the flag pole. 3. Too many sweets will make you *fat*. 4. Please turn on the electric *fan*. 5. I heard someone *rap* on the door. 6. The maple trees are full of *sap*. 7. Did you ever watch a *sham* battle? 8. The children like bread and *jam* for supper. 9. *That* is all I have for you today. 10. Move the floor *lamp* over by the chair. 11.

LESSONS ON MOVEMENTS

I held the baby on my *lap*. 12. I shall have to keep *tab* of the lessons. 13. I felt someone *tap* me on the shoulder. 14. The wind blew my *cap* overboard. 15. We had *ham* sandwiches for lunch. 16. *Have* you ever heard the story before? 17. The corned beef *hash* was browned in the pan. 18. The office boy has gone to the baseball game with his *pal*. 19. What time will you be *back*? 20. The porter will carry the *bag* to the train. 21. We walked along the *bank* of the river. 22. We followed the road marked on the *map*. 23. You must put a two cent *stamp* on your letter.

Consonants Formed and Revealed by the Lips—(*Continued*)

F, v—Lip-to-Teeth

69. For *f*, as in "few," and *v*, as in "view," the center of the lower *lip* touches the upper *teeth*.

70.   *Movement Words*
pea *fee*—heap *eve*
pen *fen*—ebb *eff*
bat *vat*—hap *have*

71.   *Practise Words*

*f*eet	*f*un	le*f*t	o*ff*
*f*ed	*f*arm	ha*v*e	cou*gh*
*f*at[1]	*f*ood	cli*ff*	ser*v*e[2]
*f*ad[1]	*f*oot	lo*v*es	sur*f*[2]
*v*an[1]	*f*ought	car*v*e	fi*v*e[3]
*f*ib	lea*v*e	roo*f*	fi*f*e[3]

72.   *Sentences*

1. The room is twenty-five *feet* wide and fifteen feet long. 2. The children *fed* the animals at the zoo. 3. There is too much *fat* on the meat. 4. Some people take up every *fad* that comes along. 5. The moving *van* will not hold all the furniture. 6. Have you ever told a *fib?* 7. It will be *fun* to go to the movies this evening. 8. Did you ever live on a *farm?* 9. How much *food* is there in the ice box? 10. We drove to the *foot* of the mountain. 11. The boys *fought* for a place on the football team. 12. The train will *leave* in five minutes. 13. I *left* my umbrella at home. 14. *Have* you ever been abroad? 15. We climbed to the top of the *cliff*. 16. Almost everyone *loves* a baby. 17. Will you *carve* the roast beef for me? 18. We were glad to have a *roof* over our heads during

the storm. 19. The boys dived *off* the bow of the boat. 20. You must do something for your *cough*. 21. What time will you *serve* dinner? 22. Can you hear the roar of the *surf* on the beach? 23. There are *five* rooms in the apartment. 24. The school has a *fife* and drum corps.

Wh, w—Puckered-Variable

73. For *wh,* as in "what," and *w,* as in "wet," the lips are drawn together or *puckered;* the degree of puckering is *variable,* being greater in slow and careful speech, and less in rapid colloquial utterance. The consonants *wh* and *w* occur only before vowels.

74.   *Movement Words*

pea fee wee
pen fen when
pack fag whack

75.   *Practise Words*

weave	whip[1]	wool	way
wheel	whim[1]	wood	wipe
web	won[2]	wall	white
well	one[2]	wharf	wove
wag	what	wave	

76. *Sentences*

1. I watched them *weave* the rug on the loom. 2. Will you take the *wheel* of the car for awhile? 3. The fly is caught in the spider's *web*. 4. There is a very deep *well* on the farm. 5. The dog will *wag* his tail if you speak to him. 6. The wind will *whip* the lake into white caps. 7. That is just a passing *whim* of mine. 8. Who *won* the prize at the bridge party? 9. I must be back at the office by *one* o'clock. 10. *What* time is it? 11. You will need a *wool* dress for the boat trip. 12. Where shall I find more *wood* for the fire? 13. We do not want many pictures on the *wall*. 14. How many boats are tied up at the *wharf?* 15. I was swept off my feet by a huge *wave*. 16. We walked all the *way* home. 17. Will you *wipe* the dishes for me? 18. Have you ever seen the *White* House in Washington? 19. The spider *wove* a web across the window.

Relaxed Vowels

Short ĭ—Relaxed–Narrow

77. For the sound of short ĭ, as in "pit," the lips have the natural or *relaxed* movement, and the opening between the lips is *narrow*.

LESSONS ON MOVEMENTS 111

78. *Movement Words*

peat pit—heap hip
feet fit—eve if
wheat wit

79. *Contrast Words*

Notice the difference between the relaxed and the extended lips.

if—eve   fill—feel
biff—beef   whip—weep

80. *Practise Words*

pill[1]	rim[2]	tip[4]	witch[5]
bill[1]	sip	dip[4]	spill
mill[1]	ship[3]	give	spin
fill	chip[3]	whiff	pick[6]
will	this	miss	big[6]
rip[2]	live	wish[5]	mink[6]

81. *Sentences*

1. There is only one *pill* left in the bottle. 2. Can you change a five dollar *bill* for me? 3. How many men work in the *mill?* 4. You may *fill* my place on the program. 5. The child has a very strong *will.* 6. How did you *rip* your

sleeve? 7. My glasses have a tortoise shell *rim*. 8. You should *sip* the water and not drink it too fast. 9. Are you waiting for your *ship* to come in? 10. Have you a *chip* on your shoulder? 11. *This* will be all for today. 12. How long would you like to *live*? 13. How did you happen to *tip* over the glass of water? 14. Would you like a *dip* in the ocean this morning? 15. How much time did you *give* to your lesson? 16. I caught a *whiff* of perfume from the rose. 17. We shall *miss* you when you leave. 18. You may have anything you *wish*. 19. She looks just like a *witch!* 20. Did you *spill* any water on the rug? 21. I should like a *spin* over the country roads. 22. Where did you *pick* up the old furniture? 23. There is a *big* crowd on the street. 25. My new coat has a *mink* collar and cuffs.

Short ŭ—Relaxed–Medium

82. For the sound of short *ŭ*, as in "but," the lips are *relaxed*, and the opening between the lips is neither narrow nor wide, but is *medium*.

LESSONS ON MOVEMENTS

83.   *Movement Words*

bit b*u*t—hip h*u*p
fin f*u*n—if h*u*ff
win w*o*n
bet b*u*t—ebb h*u*b
fen f*u*n—ĕff h*u*ff
when w*o*n

84.   *Contrast Words*

Notice that the lips are more open for short ŭ than for short ĭ.

rub—rib   love—live
sun—sin   tuck—tick

Also notice the difference between relaxed and extended lips.

dull—dell   lug—leg
rust—rest   just—jest

85.   *Practise Words*

p*u*mp[1]	s*u*m	dove[4]	m*u*sh[6]
b*u*mp[1]	sh*u*n[3]	young	m*u*ch[6]
f*u*dge	sh*u*t[3]	c*u*p[5]	d*u*ll
w*o*n	th*u*mb	come[5]	r*u*n
r*u*b[2]	love	h*u*ll	l*u*ck[7]
r*u*m[2]	tough[4]	*u*p	l*u*g[7]

86. *Sentences*

1. Will you bring me some water from the *pump*? 2. The boats *bump* against the wharf when the wind blows. 3. I made some chocolate *fudge* for you. 4. Who *won* the cup in the golf tournament? 5. You should not *rub* the cat's fur the wrong way. 6. I believe that boat is a *rum*-runner. 7. We paid a large *sum* for the house. 8. You should not *shun* your friends when they are in trouble. 9. Will you please *shut* the window for me? 10. The children *thumb* the pages of their books. 11. All is fair in *love* and war. 12. The beefsteak was very *tough*. 13. Every morning a *dove* flies to my window to be fed. 14. *Young* people are always ready for fun. 15. Will you have a *cup* of coffee for breakfast? 16. What time will you *come* for the next lesson? 17. Please *hull* the strawberries for lunch. 18. What time did you get *up* this morning? 19. Will you have sugar and cream on your *mush*? 20. There is too *much* work for one person to do. 21. There has not been a *dull* moment all day. 22. How far can you *run* without getting out of breath? 23. I was out of *luck* that time. 24. That bag is too heavy for you to *lug*.

LESSONS ON MOVEMENTS

Ah—Relaxed—Wide

87. For the sound of *ah,* as in "cart," the lips are *relaxed* and the opening between the lips is the widest of the relaxed vowels.

88. *Movement Words*

bid bud b*a*rd—hip hup h*a*rp
fin fun f*a*r—give cuff c*a*rve
bad b*a*rd—ham h*a*rm
fat f*a*r—have c*a*rve

89. *Practise Words*

p*a*rt[1]	t*a*r	sc*a*rf	he*a*rth
b*a*rn[1]	c*a*lm	f*a*r	c*a*rt[5]
f*a*rm	y*a*rd	b*a*rs[3]	c*a*rd[5]
ps*a*lm	h*a*rm	M*a*rs[3]	p*a*rk[6]
sh*a*rp	p*a*lm[2]	m*a*rsh[4]	b*a*rk[6]
l*a*rk	b*a*lm[2]	M*a*rch[4]	d*a*rk

90. *Sentences*

1. What *part* did you have in the play? 2. The *barn* has been made into a garage. 3. Have you ever lived on a *farm?* 4. Do you know the twenty-third *psalm?* 5. You must watch for the *sharp* turn in the road. 6. A

meadow *lark* flew up from the grass. 7. The men are putting *tar* on the roads. 8. The ocean is very *calm* this morning. 9. The children are playing in the back *yard*. 10. We do not want anything to *harm* the birds. 11. Will you read my *palm* for me? 12. There is *balm* in the spring air today. 13. The colors of the *scarf* are a perfect match for the suit. 14. How *far* is the golf club from your home? 15. I played over a few *bars* of the music. 16. How far is it from the earth to *Mars?* 17. We found the flowers near the *marsh*. 18. We are going South the fifth of *March*. 19. Will you sweep the ashes from the *hearth?* 20. The children have gone for a ride in the pony *cart*. 21. What address shall I put on the Christmas *card?* 22. Where shall we *park* the car? 23. The dog's *bark* is worse than his bite. 24. There is not a *dark* room in the house.

Consonants Formed by the Tongue and Revealed by the Lips

R (Before a Vowel)—Puckered–Corners
R (After a Vowel)—Puckered–Corners, or no movement

91. For *r*, as in "reef," before a vowel, the lips show a drawing together or *puckering* at the *corners*. After a vowel, as in "arm," *r*, tends to be slurred and will often show no movement whatever; though if more carefully pronounced it will show a *puckering* at the *corners*.

92. *Movement Words*

  feed weed reed
  fed wed red
  fag wag rag
  fin win rid
  fun won run
  far what rah

93. *Contrast Words*

Notice the slightly larger mouth opening for r and the greater degree of puckering for *wh* and *w*.

  reap—weep rip—whip
  rest—west run—won
    rack—whack

94. *Practise Words*

*r*ead	*r*ough	b*r*oom	fi*r*e
*r*ed	*r*aw	fea*r*	wea*r*
*r*ap[1]	*r*olls	chai*r*	*r*ope
w*r*ap[1]	f*r*esh	tho*r*n	*r*ipe
*r*amp[1]	b*r*ief	sou*r*	*r*ain
*r*ich	b*r*ush	showe*r*	wo*r*th

95. *Sentences*

1. How long will it take you to *read* the book? 2. My love is like a *red,* red rose. 3. I did not hear anyone *rap* on the door. 4. My evening *wrap* is not very warm. 5. There is a long *ramp* from the ferry to the trains. 6. Everyone in the neighborhood is very *rich.* 7. The road over the mountain was steep and *rough.* 8. The March winds are often cold and *raw.* 9. The *rolls* have just come out of the oven. 10. May I open the window for some *fresh* air? 11. I carried the papers in a *brief* case. 12. You should take the clothes out of doors to *brush* them. 13. A new *broom* sweeps clean. 14. The children have no *fear* of the dark. 15. Where shall I put your *chair?* 16. There is not a *thorn* on the rose bush. 17. Are

the oranges very *sour?* 18. We had a *shower* this afternoon. 19. It is cold enough for a *fire* in the furnace. 20. What shall I *wear* to the reception? 21. She wore a *rope* of pearls around her neck. 22. The peaches are *ripe* enough to pick. 23. Do you think it will *rain* before morning? 24. That man is *worth* a million dollars.

S, z, c (soft)—*Extended–Narrow*

96. For s, as in "saw," z, as in "zone," and c, (soft), as in "peace," the teeth are very close together, closer than for any other sound; the lips are *extended* and the opening is *narrow*. The movement, on the whole, is similar to that for long $\bar{e}$. The muscles just outside the mouth are drawn, or tightened, and this sometimes causes a slight tremulous movement there.

97.   *Movement Words*
weed reed seed
wed red said
wag rag sag
win rid sin
won run son
what rah sard

98.   *Practise Words*

seam[1]	son	piece[3]	pause[4]
seem[1]	sun	dress	paws[4]
set[2]	*starve	bus	pace
sent[2]	soup	fuss	mice
cent[2]	soon	farce	pose
sash	saw	moose	cows
sift	peace[3]	puss	boys

99.   *Sentences*

1. Will you sew the *seam* on the machine for me? 2. You *seem* very much better this morning. 3. We watched the sun *set* behind the mountain. 4. I *sent* the package to you by messenger. 5. I haven't a *cent* in my pocket. 6. The window *sash* needs a coat of paint. 7. How many times must I *sift* the flour? 8. There is only one *son* in the family. 9. The *sun* shines in every room in the house. 10. Small boys are always *starved.** 11. What kind of *soup* would you like for dinner? 12. How *soon* do you sail for Europe? 13. We *saw* all of our old friends at the reunion. 14. I am at *peace* with all the world. 15. I shall have to *piece*

---

* It is permissable to add *d*, *s* or *ed* in order to make a more natural sentence, provided the word is not being used as a homophene.

the dress to make it long enough. 16. Have I time to *dress* before dinner? 17. How much is the fare on the *bus?* 18. Don't make so much *fuss* over nothing. 19. The play was a very clever *farce*. 20. I saw the *moose* come out of the woods. 21. *Puss* likes to sleep in front of the fire. 22. There was a *pause* in the conversation. 23. The dog's muddy *paws* left marks on the porch. 24. That *pace* is too fast for me. 25. Why are women afraid of *mice?* 26. Will you *pose* for the picture? 27. The *cows* have been turned into the pasture. 28. The *boys* are making too much noise.

Sh, zh, ch, j and soft *g—Lips–Projected*
(Before a Vowel)

100. For *sh,* as in "sham," *zh,* as in "azure," (the *z* has the sound of *zh*), *ch,* as in "chap," *j,* as in "jam," and soft *g,* as in "gem," the lips are thrust forward or *projected*.

101. *Movement Words*

reed seat *sh*eet—ease ea*ch*
red said *sh*ed—ess e*dg*e
rag sag *sh*ag—has ha*sh*

102. *Contrast Words*

Notice that though the lips project for both movements, the projection is less for *r*; and also notice that for *r* the corners of the mouth are drawn down.

*s*heep—*r*eap	*s*hip—*r*ip
*s*hed—*r*ed	*s*hove—*r*uff
*j*am—*r*am	*s*hy—*r*ye

103. *Practise Words*

*s*heet	*j*ump	*J*une[2]	*ch*ains
*sh*ed	*sh*arp[1]	*sh*ook	*sh*ine
*sh*aft	*ch*arm[1]	*j*aw	*j*oin
*ch*ill	*ch*ute[2]	*sh*ow	

104. *Sentences*

1. She was as white as a *sheet* when she came into the room. 2. We had to *shed* our heavy coats while walking. 3. Have you ever been down the *shaft* of a mine? 4. There is a *chill* in the air this morning. 5. Who won the broad-*jump* at the track meet? 6. The car made a *sharp* turn to the right. 7. Some people have a great deal of *charm*. 8. Will you drop the letter down the mail *chute* for me? 9. All the

LESSONS ON MOVEMENTS 123

roses will be in bloom in *June*. 10. The storm frightened me when it *shook* the house. 11. The man has a very firm *jaw*. 12. Will you *show* me what you want me to do? 13. Should we use *chains* on the car in snowy weather? 14. The bootblack at the corner gives a wonderful *shine*. 15. Will you *join* us for supper after the theatre?

Sh, zh, ch, j and soft *g—Lips–Projected*
(After a Vowel)

105. *Movement Words*

rick sick *ch*ick—is it*ch*
run sun *sh*un—us hu*sh*
rah sard *sh*ard—ars ar*ch*

106. *Contrast Words*

sheep—seem	peach—peace
jam—sap	dredge—dress
chin—sin	mush—muss

107. *Practise Words*

rea*ch*	pat*ch*[1]	har*sh*[2]	pa*g*e
e*dg*e	pit*ch*	bu*sh*	poa*ch*
ma*sh*	ru*sh*	por*ch*	
ba*dg*e[1]	ar*ch*[2]	bir*ch*	

108. *Sentences*

1. We tried to *reach* home before the storm broke. 2. Be careful not to go too near the *edge* of the precipice. 3. The farmer made a bran *mash* for the cattle. 4. Everyone at the convention wore a *badge*. 5. Can the workman *patch* the roof before it rains? 6. The boat will toss and *pitch* when the ocean is rough. 7. I am in a *rush* to catch the train. 8. The rainbow made an *arch* in the sky. 9. The speaker had a very *harsh* voice. 10. The lilac *bush* is in full bloom. 11. There is a sleeping *porch* at the back of the house. 12. The white *birch* is one of our most beautiful trees. 13. Who tore the *page* out of the book? 14. Shall I *poach* the eggs for your breakfast?

DOUBLE CONSONANTS
Pl, bl; pr, br

109. *Movement Words*

*pl*ea pea; *pl*ay pay; *bl*ack back; *bl*ink big; *pl*ug pug; *pl*y pie; *bl*ew boo; *pl*aw paw.

*br*ee bee; *br*ay bay; *br*at bat; *pr*ick pick; *br*ung bug; *pr*y pie; *br*ook book; *br*aw paw.

LESSONS ON MOVEMENTS

110. *Practise Words*

*p*lay	*b*lew	*p*lume[1]	*p*ride
*p*ly	*b*lind	*b*lame	*b*rave
*p*lea	*b*link	*b*lank	*p*rove
*b*low	*b*loom[1]	*b*lend	*p*roud
			*b*rown

111. *Sentences*

1. Did you see the *play* last night? 2. The ship will *ply* between New York and Southampton. 3. We are ready to listen to your *plea*. 4. Which way does the wind *blow?* 5. The papers *blew* out of the window. 6. The children like to play *blind* man's buff. 7. The strong light made me *blink*. 8. Have you seen the Japanese cherry trees in *bloom?* 9. She wore a long *plume* on her hat. 10. Who was to *blame* for the accident? 11. Please fill out the order *blank* for me. 12. Water and oil will not *blend*. 13. Some people *pride* themselves on their possessions. 14. We shall have to *brave* the storm. 15. Can you *prove* that you are right? 16. We are *proud* of our country. 17. The leaves of the tree turn *brown* in the fall.

Fl, fr

112. *Movement Words*

*fl*ee fee; *fl*ay fay; *fl*ag fag; *fl*ip fib; *fl*ush fudge; *fl*y fie; *fl*aw faw.

*fr*ee fee; *fr*ay fay; *fr*ank fag; *fr*ill fill; *fr*ont fun; *fr*y fie; *fr*aw faw.

113. *Practise Words*

*fl*y	*fl*ee	*fr*ill	*fr*ont
*fl*ag	*fl*ing	*fr*ank	*fr*uit
*fl*ood	*fl*ed	*fr*esh	*fr*y
*fl*ew	*fr*ee	*fr*aud	
*fl*oor	*fr*ay	*fr*eak	

114. *Sentences*

1. We shall *fly* from New York to Montreal. 2. The *flag* is flying in the breeze. 3. Many homes were swept away by the *flood*. 4. Many of the birds *flew* South last week. 5. The office is on the fifth *floor* of the building. 6. We had to *flee* before the storm. 7. The boys must have their *fling*. 8. The burglars *fled* before the po-

lice arrived. 9. Will you have any *free* time this afternoon? 10. We are all ready for the football *fray*. 11. How do you like dresses that are trimmed with *frills*? 12. You have been *frank* about everything. 13. A *fresh* wind from the west has just sprung up. 14. The *fraud* was not discovered until it was too late. 15. A *freak* storm blew the house over. 16. Shall we sit on the *front* porch? 17. Shall I poach the eggs or shall I *fry* them? 18. *Fruit* is very plentiful this summer.

Sl, sw

115. *Movement Words*

*sl*ee see; *sl*ay say; *sl*ag sag; *sl*ick sick; *sl*ung sung; *sl*y sigh; *sl*aw saw.

*sw*ee we; *sw*ay way; *sw*ag wag; *sw*ig wig; *sw*ung won; *sw*ine wine; *sw*aw waw.

116. *Practise Words*

*sl*eep	*sl*oop	*sw*eep	*sw*erve
*sl*am	*sl*ice	*sw*ay	*sw*ing
*sl*im[1]	*sl*ate	*sw*arms	*sw*ell
*sl*ip[1]	*sl*eet	*sw*eet	
*sl*ope	*sl*ush	*sw*im	

117. *Sentences*

1. How many hours do you *sleep* every night? 2. I thought you were going to make a grand *slam* that time. 3. She is as *slim* as a young girl. 4. Small rugs are apt to *slip* on a waxed floor. 5. The hill has a gradual *slope*. 6. The boys are out sailing in their *sloop*. 7. Can you *slice* the bread very thin? 8. The house has a *slate* roof. 9. The *sleet* storm made everything look like fairyland. 10. The snow is nothing but *slush*. 11. We do not *sweep* the rugs with a broom any more. 12. Did you watch the trees *sway* in the wind? 13. There are *swarms* of mosquitoes in the country. 14. Two lumps of sugar will make the coffee too *sweet* for me. 15. How far can you *swim?* 16. I saw the car *swerve* to one side of the road. 17. We have put up a *swing* for the children. 18. The damp weather makes the doors *swell* and stick.

PUCKERED VOWELS

Long o͞o—Puckered–Narrow

118. For the sound of long *o͞o*, as in "coon," the lips are drawn together or *puckered*, and the opening between the lips is very narrow.

LESSONS ON MOVEMENTS

119. *Movement Words*

beet bit boot—heap hip whom
feet fit foot—eve if hoof
wheat wit wooed
read rid rude
seen sin soon—ease is ooze
cheat chin chew—teach dish

120. *Practise Words*

pool	soup	loom	whose
fool	soon	loon	tooth
food	shoe[1]	tomb	spool
rule	chew[1]	coop	spoon
rude	juice	whom	stool
roof	loop	proof	stoop

121. *Sentences*

1. The water in the *pool* is as clear as crystal. 2. A *fool* and his money are soon parted. 3. We must take enough *food* to camp to last for a week. 4. It is a poor *rule* that does not work both ways. 5. It was very *rude* of them to leave so soon. 6. The *roof* of the house is covered with snow. 7. What kind of *soup* would you like for dinner? 8. It will *soon* be time to

leave for the station. 9. My *shoes* were not heavy enough for walking. 10. I hope that you never *chew* gum. 11. Will you have a glass of orange *juice* for breakfast? 12. Would you be afraid to *loop* the loop? 13. We saw a ship *loom* up out of the fog. 14. Did you ever hear the cry of the *loon?* 15. Have you seen the *tomb* of Washington at Mount Vernon? 16. The chickens have been shut up in the *coop*. 17. *Whom* do you wish to see? 18. The *proof* of the pudding is in the eating. 19. *Whose* pictures are on exhibition this week? 20. The baby has only one *tooth*. 21. The wire was wound on a wooden *spool*. 22. That man was born with a silver *spoon* in his mouth. 23. You can rest better with your feet on a foot*stool*. 24. You will have to *stoop* when you go through the old doorway.

Short o͝o—Puckered–Medium

122. For the sound of short *o͝o*, as in "good," the lips are *puckered*, and the opening between the lips is neither narrow nor wide, but is *medium*.

123. *Movement Words*

        boot book
        food foot
        wooed wood
        rude rook
soon sook—booze puss
        shoot shook

        bet but put
        fen fun foot
        wen won wood
        reck rug rook
shed shun shook—mesh mush push
set sun sook—Bess bus puss

124. *Contrast Words*

Notice the greater degree of puckering for long $\bar{oo}$.

foot—food	pull—pool
put—boot	full—fool
wood—wooed	good—coot

125. *Practise Words*

p*u*ll[1]	soot	hook	p*u*t
b*u*ll[1]	shook	p*u*ss	book
f*u*ll	look	p*u*sh[3]	wolf
w*oo*d[2]	took	b*u*sh[3]	sho*u*ld
w*ou*ld[2]	cook	wool	foot

126. *Sentences*

1. You will have to *pull* the sled up the hill. 2. The *bull* fight is the national sport of Spain. 3. The hotel is *full* for the week-end. 4. Who will chop the *wood* for the stove? 5. What *would* you do if you were in my place? 6. The air of the City is filled with *soot*. 7. The wind *shook* the house during the storm. 8. *Look* up—not down; look forward—not backward. 9. I *took* the book back to the library. 10. We *cook* on an electric stove. 11. Will you bait the fish *hook* for me? 12. *Puss* always comes to the door to meet me. 13. Will you *push* the door open for me? 14. The rose *bush* is covered with blossoms. 15. Are you sure the cloth is all *wool?* 16. Where have you *put* my coat and hat? 17. I sat up until late to finish the *book.* 18. The *wolf* is at the door. 19. I *should*

have known better than to do that. 20. He put his *foot* in it that time.

Aw, o in "Orb"—Puckered-Wide

127. For the sounds of *aw,* as in "cawed," and of the *o,* in "orb," the lips are slightly *puckered,* and the opening between the lips is the *widest* of the *puckered* vowels.

128.   *Movement Words*

boot put p*aw*n—whom *o*rb
food foot f*aw*n—hoof c*o*ugh
      wooed wood w*a*lk
      rude rook r*aw*
soon sook s*ou*ght—booze puss p*au*se
shoot shook short—push porch

pat part p*aw*n—hap arm *o*rb
fat far f*aw*n—gaff carve c*o*ugh
      whack what w*a*lk
      rack rah r*aw*
sad sard s*ou*ght—as ars *aw*es
shad shard short—patch parch porch

129. Contrast Words

Notice the difference between puckered and relaxed lips.

>   for—far   born—bard
>   form—farm   orb—arm

130. Practise Words

pawn[1]	thought	caught	pall[3]
bought[1]	lawn	hall	ball[3]
form	tall	orb	maul[3]
warm	taught[2]	wharf	ought
raw	dawn[2]	gauze	hawk
short	yawn	torch	

131. Sentences

1. The stolen goods were found in a *pawn* shop. 2. We have *bought* a supply of coal for the winter. 3. The men on the baseball team are in fine *form*. 4. We have had a very *warm* summer. 5. The weather was cold and *raw* last week. 6. Do you think the dress is too *short?* I *thought* the proposition was a fair one. 8. The *lawn* was as smooth as velvet. 9. The boy

is as *tall* as his father. 10. How many years have you *taught* school? 11. I got up before *dawn* this morning. 12. It makes me sleepy to see you *yawn*. 13. We *caught* enough fish for supper. 14. All the bedrooms open onto a square *hall*. 15. The moon is the *orb* of night. 16. Will you walk down to the *wharf* with me? 17. The material was as thin as *gauze*. 18. We have an electric *torch* in the automobile. 19. There is a heavy *pall* of smoke over the town. 20. Are you going to the fancy dress *ball*? 21. You should not *maul* the puppies. 22. What do you think I *ought* to do today? 23. Why do you watch me like a *hawk*?

Consonants Formed and Revealed by the Tongue

Th—Tongue-to-Teeth

132. For *th,* as in "thin," and "then," the point of the *tongue* shows either between the *teeth* or just behind the upper *teeth*.

133. *Movement Words*

see she *th*ee—tease teach tee*th*
said shed *th*en—ĕss edge ĕth
sad shad *th*at—has hash ha*th*
suck shuck. *th*ug—us hush. do*th*
ars arch hear*th*
sort short *th*ought

134. *Practise Words*

*th*ief	*th*aw	*th*orn	hear*th*
*th*resh	*th*ought	*th*ird	boo*th*
*th*atch	*th*ink ²	tee*th*	nor*th*
*th*in	*th*ick ²	brea*th*	*th*ree
*th*umb ¹	*th*read	pi*th*	wor*th*
*th*ump ¹	*th*row	ber*th*	fif*th*

135. *Sentences*

1. A *thief* broke into the house while we were away. 2. The men will *thresh* the wheat to-morrow. 3. The house has a *thatched* roof. 4. Your coat is too *thin* for this cold weather. 5. My fingers are all *thumbs* today. 6. I heard something fall on the floor with a loud *thump*.

7. This warm weather will soon *thaw* the ice. 8. Have you *thought* about plans for a vacation? 9. Do you *think* you will go South this winter? 10. How *thick* is the ice in the river? 11. We had to *thread* our way through the traffic. 12. You should *throw* away the old newspapers. 13. I pricked my finger on the rose *thorn*. 14. This is the *third* time I have spoken to you. 15. The boy's *teeth* are in perfect condition. 16. I am out of *breath* from running. 17. That is the *pith* of the story. 18. I always try to get a lower *berth* on the sleeper. 19. There is a fire on the *hearth*. 20. I shall have to telephone from a *booth*. 21. What time in the spring do the birds fly *north?* 22. There are *three* roads leading to the house. 23. The property is not *worth* the price asked for it. 24. The shops on *Fifth* Avenue are famous all over the world.

L—Pointed-tongue-to-Gum

136. For *l*, as in "leaf," the *point* of the *tongue* touches the upper gum. The movement is seen as the tongue leaves the gum.

137. *Movement Words*

she thee *l*ee—teach teeth dea*l*
shed then *l*et—edge ĕth e*ll*
shad that *l*ad—hash hath Ha*l*
chick thick *l*ick—myth mi*ll*
shuck thug *l*uck—hush doth hu*ll*
shard *l*ard—harsh hearth Car*l*
shook *l*ook—push pu*ll*
short thought *l*ord—north ta*ll*

138. *Practise Words*

*l*eap	*l*arge	fe*ll*	wa*ll*
*l*edge	*l*oose[3]	pa*l*	whi*l*e
*l*ash[1]	*l*ose[3]	thri*ll*	who*l*e
*l*atch[1]	*l*ook	gu*ll*	bow*l*
*l*ift[2]	*l*aw	snar*l*	scow*l*
*l*ived[2]	fee*l*[4]	coo*l*	boi*l*
*l*ump	vea*l*[4]	pu*ll*	lu*ll*

139. *Sentences*

1. I saw a fish *leap* over the falls. 2. We sat on a *ledge* of rock and watched the waterfall. 3. There was danger that the waves

would *lash* the boat to pieces. 4. Be sure to *latch* the door when you leave. 5. We had to *lift* the boat over the rocks. 6. How long have you *lived* in New York? 7. The story brought a *lump* to my throat. 8. The house is much too *large* for the family. 9. I use a *loose*-leaf notebook. 10. Where did you *lose* your pocketbook? 11. We had to *look* in several stores to find what we wanted. 12. Everyone should obey the *law*. 13. Do you *feel* too much air from the window? 14. We had roast *veal* for dinner last night. 15. How much rain *fell* this month? 16. Every boy likes to have a *pal*. 17. The trip in the airplane gave me a *thrill*. 18. A sea *gull* followed our ship for many miles. 19. I was afraid to pass the dog when I heard him *snarl*. 20. The weather has been delightfully *cool* this week. 21. Who will *pull* the automobile out of the ditch? 22. The boys climbed over the *wall* for applies. 23. What shall we do to *while* away the time? 24. We had the *whole* day to ourselves. 25. Shall we *bowl* for an hour before lunch? 26 The bright light made me *scowl*. 27. We must *boil* the water for tea. 28. The *lull* in the storm lasted for only a few minutes.

T, d, n—Flat-tongue-to-Gum
(Before a Vowel)

140. For *t*, as in "tie," *d*, as in "die," and *n*, as in "nigh," the *flat* edge of the *tongue* touches the upper *gum*. The teeth are close together, which makes the tongue movement a difficult one to see; sometimes reliance must be had upon the context.

141. *Movement Words*

thee lee *t*ea—*t*ee*t*h *d*eal *d*ee*d*
*t*hen let *t*en—ĕ*t*h ell E*d*
*t*ha*t* la*d* *t*an—ha*t*h Hal ha*t*
*t*hug luck *t*uck—*d*o*t*h hull hu*t*

142. *Contrast Words*

Notice the wider lip and teeth opening for *l*, and that the tongue shows more for *l* than for *t, d,* or *n*.

tea—lee   meet—meal
dive—life   white—while
dove—love   hut—hull
turn—learn   pert—pearl
noon—loon   food—fool

LESSONS ON MOVEMENTS 141

143.   *Practise Words*

*d*eep	*d*ish[1]	*d*ump[2]	talk
*d*ebt	*d*itch [1]	*d*umb[2]	*n*ame
*d*ash	tub[2]	tool	time

144.   *Sentences*

1. Can you swim better in *deep* water than in shallow? 2. The *debt* will be paid with interest. 3. You will have to make a *dash* for your car. 4. The *dish* belonged to my grandmother. 5. There was a wide *ditch* beside the road. 6. Please fill the *tub* with hot water. 7. Where shall I *dump* the ashes? 8. I was *dumb* with fright. 9. The workman is expert in using his *tools*. 10. You gave us an interesting *talk* this morning. 11. Your *name* is hard to pronounce. 12. Have we *time* for another game of bridge?

T, d, n—Flat Tongue-to-Gum
   (After a Vowel)

145.   *Movement Words*

lark *d*ark—hearth Carl cart
look took—pull put
thought lawn *d*awn—*n*orth tall taut

146. *Contrast Words*

Notice that though the teeth are close together for both movements, they are closer for *s,* and *z,* than for *t, d, n;* that the tongue is not visible for *s,* and *z* while for *t, d, n* it may be seen as it touches the upper gum.

team—seem	peat—peace
tie—sigh	mite—mice
ton—son	mud—muss
turf—surf	pert—purse
tooth—sooth	moot—moose

147. *Practise Words*

fee*t*	fi*t*	foo*t*	bai*t*
frie*nd*	mu*d*	moo*n*	fi*ne*
pla*n*	par*t*	brough*t*	mo*de*

148. *Sentences*

1. George Washington was more than six *feet* tall. 2. I should like to meet your *friend*. 3. Have you made any *plans* for the summer? 4. Your new suit is a perfect *fit*. 5. The automobile was stuck in the *mud*. 6. Which *part* of the chicken do you like best? 7. The *moon* will be full tonight. 8. We crossed the river

by a *foot*-bridge. 9. I have *brought* you some flowers from my garden. 10. Where shall we find *bait* for fishing? 11. How large a *fine* did you have to pay? 12. The fastest *mode* of transportation is by airplane.

Double Consonants
Sl, st, thr

149.   *Movement Words*

*sl*ee lee; *sl*ay lay; *sl*ick lick; *sl*ug lug; *sl*y lie; *sl*aw law.

*thr*ee thee; *thr*ay they; *thr*ash than; *thr*ill thill; *thr*um thumb; *thr*ive thy; *thr*aw thaw.

150.   *Practise Words*

*sl*ippers	hu*st*le	fir*st*	*thr*ow
*sl*ouchy	*st*ipple	thir*st*	*thr*ush
*sl*ang	*st*ripe	*thr*ough	*thr*ob
mus*cl*e	*st*ream	*thr*ong	

151.   *Sentences*

1. The evening *slippers* have very high heels.

2. An overgrown boy often has a *slouchy* walk. 3. Almost everyone uses some *slang*. 4. His *muscles* are as hard as a rock. 5. We shall have to *hustle* to finish the work on time. 6. The painters will *stipple* the walls. 7. The safety zone is marked by a *stripe* of white paint. 8. There is a steady *stream* of traffic on the road. 9. All bills will be paid on the *first* of the month. 10. Only cold water will quench my *thirst*. 11. We walked *through* the woods looking for flowers. 12. A *throng* of people watched the parade. 13. How far can you *throw* the ball? 14. I saw a brown *thrush* in the woods today. 15. We could feel the *throb* of the ship's engines all night.

Tr, dr, shr

152. *Movement Words*

*tr*ee tee; *dr*ay day; *tr*ack tack; *tr*ick tick; *tr*uck tuck; *tr*y tie; *dr*aw daw.

*shr*ee she; *shr*ay shay; *shr*ank shank; *shr*imp ship; *shr*ug shuck; *shr*ine shy.

LESSONS ON MOVEMENTS

153.   *Practise Words*

trees	drift	trail	shrine
track	true	dream	shrewd
trump	draw	shrink	shrivel
train	trunk	shrimp	shrill
drive	draft		

154.   *Sentences*

1. The streets are lined with maple *trees*. 2. There was a large crowd at the race *track* today. 3. She held a perfect no *trump* hand. 4. The *train* was an hour late in arriving. 5. The Red Cross *drive* always comes in November. 6. We let the boat *drift* down stream for an hour. 7. Is the newspaper story a *true* one? 8. We must *draw* the line somewhere. 9. A wardrobe *trunk* is easy to pack. 10. I feel a *draft* of cold air from the window. 11. We followed the *trail* up the mountain. 12. I had a vivid *dream* of home last night. 13. Will the dress *shrink* when it is washed? 14. We had *shrimp* salad for lunch. 15. The pilgrims knelt at the *shrine* of their patron saint. 16. The salesman is a *shrewd* business man. 17. The

flowers will *shrivel* up in this heat. 18. The *shrill* whistle of the boat startled me.

Diphthongs

155. The diphthongs are *ā, ī, oy, ow, ō,* and *ū*.

Each diphthong has two elements, one of which is always more emphatic and hence more noticeable than the other. It is this emphatic element that gives the eye the clue, but it is the unemphatic element that distinguishes the diphthong from the fundamental sound.

There are three diphthongs of which the *final* element is a *puckered* movement, and there are three of which the *final* element is a *relaxed* and *narrow* movement.

Diphthongs with Puckered Final Movement

Ow

156. For *ow*, as in "how," the first movement is like that for *ah,* as in "ha," the relaxed-wide; but for *ow* this relaxed-wide movement is followed by a very evident puckered movement.

157. *Contrast Words*

Notice the puckering of the lips for *ow* which *ah* does not have.

mouse—mars   doubt—dart
pout—part   cow—car
loud—lard   how—ha

158. *Practise Words*

mouth	shout	count[2]	south
found	loud	gown[2]	foul
wound	lounge	howl	spout
round	doubt[1]	hour	pound[3]
rouse	town[1]	house	pout[3]
sound	down[1]	couch	mount[3]

159. *Sentences*

1. We rowed to the *mouth* of the river. 2. We *found* the house in perfect order. 3. The road to town *wound* in and out of the hills. 4. I bought a *round* trip ticket before I left home. 5. The bugle will *rouse* everyone in camp. 6. Can you hear the *sound* of my voice at all? 7. A *shout* went up from the crowd in the street. 8. The *loud* speaker has a beautiful tone. 9. I

will meet you in the *lounge* of the hotel. 10. I do not *doubt* a word that you say. 11. What is the population of this *town?* 12. Did you walk *down*stairs or did you use the elevator? 13. Someone should *count* the people in the room. 14. Her new *gown* is very becoming. 15. I heard the dog *howl* all night. 16. We have one *hour* to wait between trains. 17. The *house* was built many years ago. 18. The *couch* is under the south window. 19. How far *south* do you plan to go? 20. I am sure that was a *foul* ball. 21. The *spout* of the teapot has been broken. 22. How much do you pay for a *pound* of coffee? 23. The baby *pouts* when he cannot have his way. 24. Will you help me *mount* the photographs?

Long ō

160. For long *ō,* as in "go," we have what may be described as a *contracting puckered* movement, beginning with a slight puckering and somewhat wide opening of the lips (like the puckered-wide for *aw*) and becoming more puckered.

LESSONS ON MOVEMENTS 149

161.   *Movement Words*

bough be*au*
vow f*oe*
wow w*oe*
rout r*o*te
sound z*o*ne—house h*o*se
shout sh*oa*t—couch c*oa*ch
thou th*ough*—mouth b*o*th
loud l*oa*d—howl h*o*le
now n*o*—out *oa*t

162.   *Practise Words*

pole[1]	load[2]	home[3]	broke
b*ow*l[1]	l*oa*n[2]	loaf	bl*ow*
f*oa*m	t*oe*	r*o*se	b*oa*t
roll	c*o*ld	r*oa*d	stroll
s*oa*p	s*o*ld	p*oa*ch	str*o*ke
sh*ow*	h*o*pe[3]	l*oa*th	p*o*ke

163.   *Sentences*

1. The telephone *pole* was blown down in the storm. 2. I had a *bowl* of bread and milk for lunch. 3. The waves are capped with *foam* this morning. 4. We had to *roll* up in a blanket

for the night. 5. What kind of *soap* do you use? 6. Which *show* would you like to see? 7. Will you help me *load* the baggage on the truck? 8. I shall have to ask the bank for a *loan*. 9. How did you happen to stub your *toe*? 10. The weather is *cold* enough for a fire in the furnace. 11. Everything in the house was *sold* at auction. 12. While there is life there is *hope*. 13. What time will you be *home* this afternoon? 14. Shall I buy a *loaf* of whole wheat bread? 15. There was a single *rose* in a vase on the table. 16. Which *road* shall we take when we go home? 17. You must not *poach* on my preserves. 18. We were *loath* to go back to the City. 19. The wind *broke* the plate glass window. 20. Which way does the wind *blow*? 21. We went around the lake in a motor *boat*. 22. Will you take a *stroll* along the beach with me? 23. Who is *stroke* of the college crew? 24. *Poke* up the fire if you want it to burn.

Long ū

164. The beginning element for long ū, as in "mute," is a very quick relaxed-narrow movement, which is followed by a very decided puckered movement, like that for long o͞o.

As a rule, the relaxed-narrow element of long ū cannot be seen after the following consonants, t, (tune), d, (due), n (new), l (lieu), s (sue), th, (thew); and then ū must be told from long o͞o by the context.

165. *Movement Words*

bough beau p*ew*—cope c*u*be
vow foe f*ew*
house hose *u*se
couch coach h*u*ge
mole m*u*le
mount mote m*u*te

166. *Practise Words*

p*ew*	cue	c*u*be	m*u*le
m*ew*	f*u*me	h*ew*	m*u*te
f*ew*[1]	n*ew*	*u*se	m*u*se
v*iew*[1]	t*u*bes	h*u*ge	

167. *Sentences*

1. How far is your *pew* from the front of the church? 2. I heard the cat *mew* for his supper.

3. We have only a *few* choice seats for the play left. 4. There is a beautiful *view* of the valley from the window. 5. The actor failed to get his *cue*. 6. Why do you fret and *fume* about everything? 7. All the furniture in the house is *new*. 8. We need new *tubes* for the radio. 9. How many sides has a *cube*? 10. The men had to *hew* their way through the forest. 11. May I *use* your telephone? 12. The new factory is a *huge* building. 13. He is as stubborn as a *mule*. 14. The violinist had to *mute* the strings of his instrument. 15. I like to *muse* before an open fire.

Consonants Revealed by Context

Y—Relaxed–Narrow

168. For *y,* as in "yea," the lips are *relaxed* and the opening between the lips is *narrow*. It is like the movement for short ĭ. The movement for *y,* however, is so quick that the eye seldom sees it; usually the sound must be revealed by the context.

Y occurs, as a consonant, only before vowels. It is not a common sound, and therefore, though difficult, it causes little trouble.

LESSONS ON MOVEMENTS

169. *Movement Words*

lee tea *y*e
let ten *y*et
lad tan *y*ak
luck tuck *y*oung
lard darn *y*arn
lawn dawn *y*awn

170. **Practise Words*

*y*east	*y*awn	*y*awl	*y*oke[2]
*y*ell	*y*arn[1]	*y*ear	*y*earn
*y*ank	*y*ard[1]	*y*elp	*y*acht
*y*oung	*y*outh	*y*olk[2]	*y*ule

171. *Sentences*

1. How many cakes of *yeast* shall I buy for you? 2. The boys always *yell* at a football game. 3. You must not *yank* the reins when you drive. 4. The children are too *young* to

---

* These words are very difficult. Do not expect too much. Be careful to say them naturally and without exaggeration.

** Remember that "usually the sound (for k, hard c, hard g, etc.) must be revealed by the context," and do not insist upon seeing these words apart from the thought of a sentence, except for mirror practise. Even then, note whatever movements are visible when the words are spoken naturally and let it go at that.

be left alone. 5. The warm weather makes me want to *yawn*. 6. I haven't enough *yarn* to finish the sweater. 7. There is a large *yard* in front of the house. 8. The enthusiasms of *youth* are often misunderstood. 9. The fishermen left this morning in a *yawl*. 10. This is the *year* for the presidential election. 11. Did you hear the *yelp* of that dog? 12. You must boil the egg until the *yolk* is hard. Did you ever see a *yoke* of oxen? 14. We often *yearn* for the comforts of home. 15. The *yacht* was built to cross the ocean. 16. We shall light the *yule* candle on Christmas Eve.

K, c (hard), *g* (hard), *ng, nk—Throat-Movement*

172. For *k*, as in "kin," hard *c*, as in "cat," hard *g*, as in "go," *ng*, as in "rang," and *nk*, as in "rank," a drawing up of the throat muscles just above the Adam's apple may sometimes be seen. The movement is slight, and if seen at all, must be seen while the eyes are on the mouth. Usually these sounds must be revealed by the context.

LESSONS ON MOVEMENTS

173. *Movement Words*

tea key—eat eke
ten get—Ed egg
tack gag—had hag
tuck cut—hut hug
darn cart—art ark
took cook—good cook
daw caw—awed auk

174. **Practise Words*

keel	coon	rang[2]	hooked
get	good	rank[2]	walk
gift	call	ring[3]	quart
cuff	leak	rink[3]	cream[4]
card[1]	peck	rug	creep[4]
cart[1]	rack		

175. *Sentences*

1. The *keel* of the boat struck a rock. 2. What time do you *get* up in the morning? 3. The *gift* is just what I wanted. 4. The *cuff* of the shirt is badly worn. 5. Are you going to

* See note on p. 153.
** See note on p. 153.

the *card* party this afternoon? 6. Did you ever buy anything from a push *cart* peddlar? 7. I wore a *coon* skin coat to the football game. 8. The men have done very *good* work on the road. 9. Shall I *call* for you on the way home? 10. Did you find the *leak* in the roof? 11. We bought a *peck* of potatoes from the farmer. 12. You may hang your hat and coat on the *rack* in the hall. 13. Who *rang* the door bell? 14. *Rank* after rank of soldiers passed by in the parade. 15. The diamond *ring* has a platinum setting. 16. How many people were at the skating *rink?* 17. There is a nine by twelve *rug* on the floor. 18. How much did you pay for the *hooked* rug? 19. I took a long *walk* before breakfast. 20. Can you drink a *quart* of milk a day? 21. The *cream* is not heavy enough to whip. 22. The baby is just beginning to *creep.*

H—Aspirate

176. For *h*, as in "hat," there is no movement. *H* has the appearance of the following vowel. It must always be told by the context.

In the following *Practise Words*, a word given without the *h*, will in each instance be homophenous to the word immediately preceding it. All words must be told by the context.

177.   *Practise Words*

heat[1]	ill[2]	hall[4]	hope[5]
eat[1]	hunt	haul[4]	hike
head	heart[3]	all[4]	hail[6]
ham	art[3]	howl	ale[6]
hill[2]	hood	home[5]	hole

178.   *Sentences*

1. The furnace will *heat* the house in the coldest weather. 2. What shall we *eat* for lunch? 3. The airplane had to battle *head* winds all the way. 4. We shall have baked *ham* for dinner. 5. The children are coasting down the *hill*. 6. I have not been *ill* for a long time. 7. The men have gone to the North Woods to *hunt* deer. 8. My *heart* was in my mouth when we drove up the mountain. 9. Will you go to the Museum of *Art* with me? 10. You will have to raise the *hood* of the car to find the trouble. 11. The *hall* is very long and narrow. 12. Someone will have to *haul* the firewood to the house. 13. We had *all* we

could do to walk against the wind. 14. Did you hear the wind *howl* last night? 15. There is no place like *home*. 16. I shall *hope* to see you before long. 17. The Boy Scouts are going on a *hike*. 18. The *hail* stones were as large as marbles. 19. Will you have a glass of *ale* with your lunch? 20. I want to play one more *hole* of golf.

Double Consonants
Gl, cl; Gr, cr

179.   *Movement Words*

*gl*ee key; *cl*ay gay; *cl*ap cap; *cl*ick kick; *cl*ub cub; *gl*ide guide; *cl*aw caw.

*cr*ee key; *gr*ay gay; *cr*ap cap; *cr*ick kick; *cr*umb come; *cr*y guy; *cr*aw caw.

180.   *Practise Words*

*gl*impse	*cl*erk	*cr*owd	*gr*avel
*cl*oud	*cl*ose	*cr*otch	*gr*owth
*cl*imbed	*gl*eam	*gr*ound	*cr*ush
*gl*ow	*gl*ove	*gr*oup	*cr*ystal
*cl*asp	*cr*edit		

LESSONS ON MOVEMENTS

181. *Sentences*

1. I caught a *glimpse* of you as you passed by. 2. There is a black *cloud* in the West. 3. We *climbed* to the top of the light house. 4. There was a beautiful after-*glow* in the sky last night. 5. The *clasp* on my purse is broken. 6. The *clerk* in the glove department was very polite. 7. The air is very *close* today. 8. We could see just a *gleam* of light through the fog. 9. Will you mend the hole in my *glove*? 10. You will be allowed *credit* up to $10,000. 11. There was a large *crowd* at the meeting. 12. There is a bird's nest in the *crotch* of the tree. 13. The *ground* is covered with snow this morning. 14. We must divide the class into *groups*. 15. I do not like to walk on a *gravel* path. 16. The *growth* of the village has been rapid. 17. You will *crush* the flowers if you carry them that way. 18. She wore a string of *crystal* beads and ear rings to match.

Diphthongs (*Continued*)

Diphthongs with Relaxed and Narrow Final Movement

Long ī

182. For long *ī*, as in "pie," the first movement is like that for *ah*, in "pa," the relaxed-wide; but for long *ī*, this relaxed-wide movement is followed by a quick relaxed-narrow movement.

183. *Contrast Words*

Contrast the sounds of long *ī* and *ah;* notice that both begin with the relaxed-wide movement, but that *ī* is followed by the relaxed-narrow, while *ah* is not.

pipe—palm	light—lard
mice—mars	dine—darn
pike—park	I'm—arm

184. *Practise Words*

p*ie*[1]	s*i*ght	t*y*pe[5]	p*i*le[6]
b*uy*[1]	sh*y*	k*i*nd	m*i*le[6]
f*i*ght[2]	sh*i*ne	w*i*pe	b*i*te[7]
f*i*ne[2]	l*i*ght[4]	d*i*ve	m*i*ght[7]
r*i*pe[3]	l*i*ne[4]	w*i*re	p*i*ne[7]
rh*y*me[3]	t*i*me[5]	w*i*se	l*i*ke

185. *Sentences*

1. The apple *pie* has just come out of the oven. 2. Where can we *buy* our supplies? 3. Boys should learn to *fight* their own battles. 4. We had to pay a $5.00 *fine*. 5. The fruit is picked and shipped before it is *ripe*. 6. Can you make up a simple *rhyme* for me? 7. We caught *sight* of the house from the road as we passed. 8. The little girl seems to be very *shy*. 9. Does that light *shine* into your eyes? 10. The *light* is too dim to read by. 11. You should sign your name on the dotted *line*. 12. There is not *time* for anything more today. 13. The book has very fine *type*. 14. It was very *kind* of you to do that for me. 15. The storm *wiped* out the entire village. 16. Do you know how to *dive?* 17. Be sure to send me a *wire* when you arrive. 18. It is not *wise* to buy the house now. 19. Our wood *pile* is getting very low. 20. We are just one *mile* from home. 21. The fish will not *bite* today. 22. We worked with *might* and main to finish in time. 23. There is a grove of white *pine* trees around the reservoir. 24. What would you *like* to have me do?

Long ā

186. For long ā, as in "late," the first movement is like that for ĕ, in "let," the extended-medium; but for long ā, this extended-medium movement is followed by a quick relaxed-narrow movement. The relaxed-narrow element is difficult to see in this diphthong; it has the effect of making ā slightly slower in formation than ĕ. Frequently, however, the two sounds must be told apart by the context.

187. *Movement Words*

pie p*ay*—I'm *a*pe
fie f*ay*—knife kn*a*ve
why w*ay*
rye r*ay*
sigh s*ay*—ice *a*ce
shy sh*ay*
thy th*ey*—tithe l*a*the
lie l*ay*—isle *a*le
nigh n*ay*—I'd *a*id
guy g*ay*—like l*a*ke
high, h*ay*

188. *Practise Words*

pa*i*l [1]	*r*a*y*	tam*e* [4]	pa*g*e
ma*i*l [1]	*s*a*v*e	ba*s*t*e*	fa*i*th
fa*i*l	*sh*am*e* [3]	a*i*m	*sh*ad*e* [6]
*v*a*i*n	*sh*ap*e* [3]	*w*a*v*e [5]	*ch*a*i*n [6]
*w*a*y* [2]	lam*e*	*w*a*i*f [5]	ba*k*e [7]
*w*e*i*gh [2]	nam*e* [4]	*r*a*c*e	ma*k*e [7]

189. *Sentences*

1. Will you bring a *pail* of water from the spring? 2. What time does the *mail* come in? 3. The work must be finished today without *fail*. 4. We made a *vain* effort to catch the train. 5. We could not find our *way* through the woods. 6. Some people *weigh* themselves every day. 7. There was hardly a *ray* of light in the room. 8. You should *save* your strength for more important things. 9. It is a *shame* for you to work so hard. 10. What is the *shape* of the room? 11. I was so *lame* I could hardly walk. 12. You have a very unusual *name*. 13. The bear cub is as *tame* as a kitten. 14. You must *baste* the seams before sewing them. 15. What is your *aim* in life? 16. The cold *wave* did not last long. 17. The little *waif* has no

home. 18. Have you ever seen a horse *race?* 19. There is a *page* torn out of the book. 20. I have unbounded *faith* in you. 21. We stood in the *shade* of the tree while we waited for the car. 22. The platinum *chain* is set with diamonds. 23. When will you *bake* fresh bread? 24. How much profit did you *make* on the sale?

Oy

190. For *oy,* as in "boy," the first movement is like that for *aw,* in "paw," the puckered-wide; but for *oy,* this puckered-wide movement is followed by a quick relaxed-narrow movement.

191. *Movement Words*

buy bay b*oy*
file fail f*oi*l—knife knave c*oif*
rye ray R*oy*
side sail s*oi*l—dice days t*oy*s
line lain l*oi*n—isle ale *oi*l
tie day t*oy*—kine cane c*oi*n
guy gay c*oy*

192. *Practise Words*

boys	join[1]	noise	broil
boil	joint[1]	coil	voice
foil	loin	coin	poise
soil	toil	oil	toys

193. *Sentences*

1. The *boys* play ball as soon as school is out. 2. We had to *boil* the coffee in a tin pot. 3. The candy was wrapped in tin *foil*. 4. The *soil* on the farm is very rich. 5. We shall *join* you on the way home. 6. The exercise made me stiff in every *joint*. 7. How many *loin* lamb chops shall I order? 8. We had to *toil* all day long to repair the road. 9. There is so much *noise* I cannot hear you. 10. The sailor *coiled* the rope on the deck of the boat. 11. How much is the *coin* worth? 12. Are you sure we have enough *oil* and gasoline? 13. Will you *broil* the beefsteak over the coals? 14. You have a very pleasant *voice*. 15. The speaker had unusual dignity and *poise*. 16. Many *toys* are made in Germany.

COLLOQUIAL FORMS, VOWEL AND CONSONANT EXERCISES AND HOMOPHENOUS WORDS

194. These lessons provide the student with the best possible training for all-around lip-reading. They give, in an advanced form, the same type of training as the preceding lessons. As the principal aim of lessons in lip-reading is to train for skill in understanding conversation, these exercises are particularly valuable. Where the speaker sticks to his subject and does not digress, the lip-reader, once he knows what it is all about, finds it fairly easy to follow. The difficulty comes in getting the subject in the first place, or following when the subject is changed suddenly, or understanding when a third person takes part in the conversation.

If the student is to be able to understand everyday conversation his mind must be trained to make use of every clue possible, whether it be the subject of the conversation, a word, a facial expression or a gesture, and there must be much training in alertness by giving sentences that are unrelated in thought. The eyes must be trained, too, to be as accurate as possible in their subconscious recognition of movements and words.

Colloquial Forms

195. It is obviously good practise to train the eyes to catch the common forms and expressions which pass from mouth to mouth again and again in a day's conversation. They may be divided into two classes, first, complete colloquial sentences, and, second, parts of sentences, forms or phrases.

The forms that are given in the lessons that follow are especially common in the asking of questions. The first few words of a question are frequently the key to the whole. To lose them means failure; to get them means success. The value of the repeated practise of these forms, thus fixing them in the visual memory, is therefore apparent.

Visual memory is not the memory that enables us to recite what we have learned, but that which enables us infallibly to recognize by sight objects or movements studied. The diamond expert takes a handful of unmounted gems and by color or form or the slightest peculiarities instantly tells one from the other; whereas the untrained eye could not pick out one in ten. It is practise in close observation that gives the eye this quickness and sharpness in recognizing the particular object, and it is just such practise that the lip-reader requires in the study of these colloquial forms.

In practising these forms before the mirror the aim should be to familiarize the eye both with the form and with the auxiliary verb that follows it. Saying the complete sentence, concentrate (but do not emphasize) on the form; then repeat the sentence and concentrate on the auxiliary verb. The order of these verbs should be arranged so as to bring together for contrast and comparison those verbs that are apt to be confused. The sentence should not be varied, except as the requirements of grammar may demand. The sentences given below will illustrate these points; the grouping of the verbs apt to be confused is indicated by the separating spaces. Go over each group with the mirror many times. This method will apply for all of the "forms." Compose for each "form" a simple sentence that can be used with

COLLOQUIAL FORMS

all the auxiliary verbs with only slight changes to make it grammatical. For example:

How long has he been here?
" " does he stay here?
" " is he to be here?

" " has he been here?
" " had he been here?
" " can he be here?

" " did he stay here?
" " is he to be here?

" " am I to be here?
" " may he be here?
" " might he be here?
" " must he be here?

" " was he to be here?
" " were you to be here?
" " will you be here?
" " would you be here?

" " would you stay here?
" " could you stay here?
" " do you stay here?

" " shall I be here?
" " should I be here?

" " have you been here?
" " are you to be here?
" " ought you to be here?

In the following lessons the questions on the Colloquial Forms are intended for mind training only. The method of home practise (in addition to mirror practise) is to have someone read the questions, the student concentrating on the *thought* of the question. He will know the "form" with which each question begins and thus have a clue to the thought. Form, verb or the question itself should not be repeated. If the question is not understood the first time, it should be repeated smoothly and naturally. If the student still does not get it, he should be given the thought in different words, or a clue word should be given, making sure that the word gives a real clue to the thought. If the question is understood, then the next one should be given quickly, as the practise of going quickly from one thought to another trains for alertness in conversation. If the student wishes to verify his understanding of the question he should answer it, rather than to repeat it. To repeat is unnatural, and it will have a tendency to lessen the student's confidence in his understanding of what is said, will tend to make him analytical, and, if the practise is continued, will form a bad mental habit that will retard, if not prevent, progress in reading the lips.

Vowel and Consonant Exercises

196. These exercises are intended for eye training, and they therefore provide particularly good material for mirror practise. It is not possible always to recognize the vowel, and many of the consonant movements, when used in natural speech, but it must be kept in mind that if any degree of accuracy of subconscious recognition is to be acquired there must be constant drill. In reading the printed page we have arbitrary symbols which do not vary, but in reading the lips the movements vary with each mouth, and with the different combinations of movement. This makes it all the more necessary to practise with the mirror and with others. While perfection is not possible, intensive practise with the mirror and with the teacher in the lessons, will bring its reward in a quicker, more accurate *subconscious* recognition of these movements.

Do not forget that when actually reading the lips, as in conversation, there must be no more thought of individual movements than there is of individual letters when reading the printed page. One interferes with thought-getting as much as the other. Let the eye training be a definite watching for certain movements and words, but when reading the lips, concentrate the entire attention on the thought of the speaker.

Vowels

197. Vowels are divided into three groups, the *puckered, relaxed* and the *extended*. Under each group we have a *narrow* opening between the lips, a *medium* opening, and a *wide* opening. See p. 85, Lessons on the Movements. As it is difficult to pronounce these vowel sounds by themselves they are classified below in words:

	Puckered	*Relaxed*	*Extended*
Narrow	coon (oo)	kid (ĭ)	keen (ē)
Medium	good (oo)	cut (ŭ)	get (ĕ)
Wide	cawed (aw)	cart (ah)	cat (ă)

When practising these words with the mirror, and the words in all of the vowel exercises that follow, *be sure to say the three words naturally and smoothly* to give the effect of natural speech. As the student repeats the words he should watch his mouth in the mirror and think of what he is trying to *see*, and also *feel* the movements as he says them, thus making use of the multiple sense of appeal. He *hears* the word as he says it; he *sees* it on the lips, and he *feels* it.

The first step in the study of these words is for the student to try them on his own mouth, watching in the mirror the formation of the vowels. Compare the formation on the lips with the description given, then proceed as follows: Say the three words of the puckered group, "coon good cawed," and watch in the mirror to see the difference between the narrow, the medium, and the wide openings. Then say the same words again in reverse order, then in several different orders, over and over, until satisfied that you have mastered theoretically at least the peculiarities of the puckered vowels. Then try the words of the relaxed group, and then those of the extended group in the same way.

Now take the three words in the narrow group, "coon, kid, keen," and watching the mouth in the mirror, observe the difference between the puckered movement, the relaxed, and the extended. Say the same words again in reverse order, then in several different orders, over and over, until you feel that you have mastered the differences between the narrow vowels. Then try the words of the medium group, and then those of the wide group similarly. Such mastery will not be accomplished in one day or ten.

The vowels in these exercises are combined with all the fundamental consonant movements, both before and after the vowels, as in the Lessons on the Movements. Practise each exercise as directed above.

Consonants

198. In the consonant exercises in the following lessons, material is given for the study of the consonant movements, both before and after the vowels and diphthongs. Take the first exercise for example:

back	fag	whack	am	have	has
fag	whack	rack	have	has	hash
whack	rack	sack	has	hash	hath
rack	sack	shack	hash	hath	Hal
sack	shack	thank	hath	Hal	hat
shack	thank	lack			
thank	lack	tack			

Study these words with the mirror in the following manner: Take the three words in the first group, "back fag whack," and observe closely the differences, which you will notice lie solely in the initial consonants, the *b, f* and *wh*. Repeat the words in direct order, reverse order and several different orders, until these consonant movements are thoroughly learned. Then practise the next group of three, "fag whack rack," in the same way, and so on with each group. Then try three words, skipping around, changing them from different groups, as "back rack thank," "lack sack whack," "shack fag tack." Then practise in the same way with the words in the right-hand groups, those with the consonant movements at the end of the words, and observe the differences in the *final* consonants of each group.

It is important that the words of a group should not be pronounced slowly, word-by-word, but rapidly, the three words together.

Homophenous Words

199. The fact that the sounds in certain consonant groups have the same visible movement gives rise to a considerable body of homophenous words,—that is, words that appear alike on the lips. The two sounds of *f* and *v* in "few" and "view" appear exactly the same when the words are spoken naturally. So do *p, b* and *m* in the words "pay," "bay," and "may."

Such words cannot be told apart by their formation unless the movements be exaggerated; and exaggeration, as has been said, is something which the student must guard against most carefully. These words must be distinguished by the thought, or context, in which they are used. For example:

There is a beautiful *view* from my window.
I have only a *few* minutes to spare before I leave.

How much did you *pay* for the house?
We have been out sailing on the *Bay* this afternoon.
How much time *may* we have for the work?

There can be no question about the difficulty of telling these words apart, as words, when spoken naturally, rapidly and without exaggeration. It is the best evidence that no eyes, no matter how well trained, could ever successfully read the lips without help from the mind. But when the words are put into sentences the mind readily supplies the right word.

COLLOQUIAL FORMS

The consonants that are homophenous are:

p, b, m (mp and mb)
f, v (ph and gh)
wh, w
s, z, soft c
sh, zh, ch, j and soft g
t, d, n (nt, nd, and ed following n when it does not form an extra syllable.)
k, c (hard), g (hard), ng, nk and ck

L has no sound of like appearance. If it appears in one word of a homophenous group it must appear in all. *H* has no movement; it is merely a breath. Therefore, *hill* and *ill* are alike.

In the vowels there are no strictly homophenous sounds, though in rapid speech long *ā* and short *ĕ* are practically impossible to distinguish except by the context. Short *ŏ* and Italian *a* (ah) differ visibly only in quantity and duration, as is also true of the o in "long," and broad *a* (aw). Long *ū* and long *ōō* are usually homophenous.

When making up, or finding, the homophenous words of a group, it must be kept in mind that all *movements* (not letters) in the words must be alike. If the word begins with *p, b* or *m,* then all other words in the group must begin with *p, b* or *m*. If the word ends with *t, d, n, nt* or *nd,* then all of the words must end with that movement. The vowels must be the same as there are no homophenous vowel sounds.

Suppose we take the word "pet" and find all of the words that are homophenous to it.

First, we shall take the *p* and short *ĕ*:

    pet, pen, pent, pend, penned

then the *b* and short *ĕ*:

    bet, bed, bend, bent

and *m* and short *ĕ*:

    met, men, mend, meant

All thirteen of these words look alike on the lips and can only be told apart by the context of the sentence.

The more familiar the lip-reader is with words of homophenous formation the better will he understand conversation. One of the things for him to do, therefore, is to *memorize* with each lesson the words that look alike. He should be able, if given one word, to recall off-hand all the other words that are like it. He should also try each group of words before the mirror, and verify on his own lips their homophenous formation. Then he should practise the sentences with the mirror, as directed for other sentence practise, and should compose as many sentences as are naturally suggested by the words. The sentence should be simple and colloquial in style and not involved; the aim should be to compose the sentences quickly and not stop to puzzle them out. Words that have more than one meaning, as, for example, "vault," should be used in separate sentences for each meaning of the word. Similarly, a word that may be either noun or verb, or noun and adjective, should be used in separate sentences for each significance.

In the following lessons one sentence only has been given for each word. The student, or his assistant, should make up other sentences.

It is splendid practise for the student to cover all but one word of a group and then try to make up the rest of the words in that group. Or to take any word and see how many homophenes he can find for the word. These should be corrected or verified by the teacher or by reference to a list of homophenous words to make sure that the student knows the homophenous formations.

The ability to quickly substitute another word with the same movements when a sentence is not understood, greatly increases the ease with which a lip-reader can follow conversation.

LESSONS ON COLLOQUIAL FORMS, VOWEL AND CONSONANT EXERCISES, AND HOMOPHENOUS WORDS

200.   HOW LONG

How long have you been here?
" " " they been abroad?
" " " we been away from home?
" " has he been working?
" " " he been out of work?
" " " it been raining?
" " had the storm lasted?
" " " they been out of town?
" " " you waited for me?
" " am I to wait for you?
" " " I to practise my lesson?
" " is the pole?
" " "the room?
" " "the table?
" " are you going to be in town?

How long are you to be on the ocean?
"   "   " they to remain in the West?
"   "   was the movie?
"   "   " the story?
"   "   " the play?
"   "   were they in the City?
"   "   " you on your vacation?
"   "   " they to be abroad this summer?
"   "   will you be away?
"   "   " they be in town?
"   "   " he keep the news to himself?
"   "   would you be willing to wait?
"   "   " you like to live abroad?
"   "   " you like to live?
"   "   shall we wait for the mail?
"   "   " I boil the eggs?
"   "   should we wait for him?
"   "   " I hold the wire?
"   "   do you think it will rain?
"   "   " they want to think the matter over?
"   "   " we stop at Buffalo?
"   "   does he expect to be gone?
"   "   " he stay abroad?
"   "   " the ship stay in the harbor?

How long did they remain South?
" " " the storm last?
" " " you wait for me?
" " may we use the phone?
" " " I keep the book?
" " " we have for study?
" " might I have to walk?
" " " we have to wait for the train?
" " can you keep a secret?
" " " you hold your breath?
" " " you swim?
" " could you keep quiet?
" " " they walk without stopping?
" " must we stay here?
" " " I practise my lesson?
" " ought we to rest?
" " " she to remain South?
" " before you will come back?
" " " she goes away?
" " ago were you in Washington?
" " since you left New York?
" " " you saw your friend?

201.   Vowel Exercise

boot	beet	bit	hōop	hip	heap
book	but	bet	hŏop (?)	up	ebb
pawn	bard	bat	orb	arm	am
food	fit	feet	hōof	if	eve
foot	fun	fed	hŏof (?)	huff	deaf
fawn	far	fat	cough	carve	have

202.   Homophenous Words

baggage, package

    This train does not carry *baggage*.

    I have mailed my last Christmas *package*.

bargain, market

    I was forced to make the best of a bad *bargain*.

    I bought these roses at the flower *market*.

baste, paste

    How often should I *baste* the roast turkey?

    Where shall I find the jar of *paste?*

brag, prank

    Small boys like to *brag* of what they can do.

    The boys are up to some Hallowe'en *prank*.

break, brake
>This storm may *break* the windows in the house.
>The *brake* of the automobile was out of order.

brown, proud
>The boy is *proud* of his record at school.
>The bride was dressed all in *brown*.

cave, gave
>The boys used the *cave* for a playhouse.
>Who *gave* the library to the town?

cereal, serial
>What *cereal* will you have for breakfast?
>The story was published first in *serial* form.

chair, share
>Where shall I put your steamer *chair*?
>You have given me more than may *share* of the lunch.

charm, sharp
>You are wearing a very unusual watch *charm*.
>There was a *sharp* drop in the prices of stocks.

203. How Much

How much have you spent for clothes this year?
" " " you saved this month?
" " " you earned this week?
" " has been paid on the bill?
" " " been done on the house?
" " " it rained this week?
" " had you heard about the play?
" " " she promised to give to the church?
" " " you hoped to make on the sale?
" " am I to receive for the day's work?
" " " I to pay for the radio?
" " " I to spend for the prizes?
" " is the railroad fare to New York (San Francisco, Chicago, etc.)
" " " the automobile to cost?
" " " a year's subscription to the magazine?
" " are you prepared to offer for the property?
" " " the apples a basket?

How much are the workmen paid for the job?
" " was left over from dinner?
" " " the work to cost?
" " " the automobile worth?
" " were we asked to give to the Christmas Fund?
" " " you at home this summer?
" " will the trip cost us?
" " " we see from the airplane?
" " " you spend for your vacation?
" " would you advise me to invest in real estate?
" " " a trip to Florida cost?
" " " the company be willing to spend for improvements?
" " water shall I put on the plants?
" " " I put aside for expenses?
" " " I charge for the use of the garage?
" " should I practise my lesson?
" " " we spend on movies each week?

COLLOQUIAL FORMS

How much should I read before my lesson?
" " do you want me to give to the Fair?
" " " you think the watch cost?
" " " the churches advertise in the papers?
" " does your doctor charge?
" " " golf take you away from business?
" " " he know about politics?
" " did you earn last month?
" " " you pay for your ticket?
" " " you make from the auction sale?
" " may I use your radio?
" " " we use the tennis courts?
" " " I use without being extravagant?
" " might we keep for our own use?
" " " I expect to receive under the will?
" " help can we get from the home office?
" " " you spend for furniture?

How much can you hear at the theatre?
" " must I do before bedtime?
" " " I pay for the theatre tickets?
" " " I allow for the journey?
" " ought to be done in the house?
" " " we to help at the Club?
" " " we to give to the Red Cap?

204. VOWEL SOUNDS

you	yin	ye
—	young	yet
yaw	yarn	yak

coon	kid	keen	duke	ink	eke
good	cut	get	cook	hug	egg
cawed	cart	cat	auk	ark	hag

205. HOMOPHENOUS WORDS

chatter, shatter

We were amused by the *chatter* of the monkeys at the Zoo.

The *shatter*-proof-glass in the windshield saved my life.

class, glass

The *class* was dismissed at three o'clock.

The students were taken on a trip through the *glass* factory.

coarse, course

The window screens are too *coarse* to keep out the mosquitos.

How many players are on the golf *course?*

cream, creep

Will you have sugar and *cream* in your coffee?

We had to *creep* over the rocks on our hands and knees.

dirt, turn

We drove for miles over a *dirt* road.

Go straight ahead until you come to the first *turn* to the right.

displace, displays

I was careful not to *displace* anything in the room.

The window *displays* on the Avenue are beautiful.

door, tore

Be sure to leave the *door* unlocked when you go out.

The wind *tore* the boat from its moorings.

drew, true

> I *drew* enough money from the bank to pay the bills.
>
> Is that a *true* story of the affair?

drink, trick

> We stopped at the farm for a *drink* of water.
>
> The dog has learned a new *trick*.

fair, fare

> Have you ever been to a County *Fair*?
>
> How much is the *fare* by train?

---

206. How Far

How far have you read in the book?
" " " we gone since morning?
" " " you walked today?
" " has the concrete road been finished?
" " " the boat drifted with the wind?
" " " the work on the house progressed?
" " had you gone when the storm broke?
" " " the wind blown your hat?
" " " you walked before I met you?
" " am I from home?
" " " I to follow you?

COLLOQUIAL FORMS 191

How far am I to drive the car?
" " is New York from San Francisco?
" " " it to the Country Club?
" " " it to the station?
" " are we to travel by boat?
" " " they going by airplane?
" " " the houses from the river?
" " was the Post Office from the house?
" " " the car parked from the curb?
" " " the golf club from the town?
" " were my instructions carried out?
" " " they from the house when it rained?
" " " they from home when they lost their way?
" " will you walk with me?
" " " his voice carry?
" " " the bus take us?
" " would you like to travel with us?
" " " you take us in your car?
" " " you like to walk?
" " shall we swim this afternoon?
" " " I follow the mountain path?
" " " we walk along the road?
" " should I be able to see with the field glasses?

How far should you think it is to the top of the mountain?
" " do you feel like walking this morning?
" " " you want me to carry the bag for you?
" " " telephone messages go?
" " does the subway take you?
" " " this boat go?
" " " the train go without stopping?
" " did you go by automobile?
" " " the police chase the thief?
" " " you throw the ball?
" " may we venture into the woods?
" " " I go with you?
" " " we walk through the building?
" " can the bird fly?
" " " Babe Ruth bat a ball?
" " " the search-light pierce the fog?
" " could they see in the snow storm?
" " " you trust that man?
" " " the road be traveled safely?
" " must we walk to play golf?
" " " the farmer drive to market?
" " " the workmen carry the lumber?
" " ought I to go with the strangers?
" " " we to be by this time?

COLLOQUIAL FORMS

How far is the North Pole from the South Pole?
" " can you see in the dark?
" " does the surface car take you?
" " do you think it is to the next town?

207. VOWEL EXERCISE

toot	tin	tea	hoot	it	eat
took	tuck	ten	hood	hut	end
dawn	tar	tan	awed	art	add

loot	lit	lean	cool	ill	eel
look	luck	let	pull	hull	ell
lawn	lard	lad	awl	Carl	Hal

208. HOMOPHENOUS WORDS

fault, vault

    It was no one's *fault* that we missed the train.

    Who holds the pole *vault* record?

few, view

    There are only a *few* apples left in the barrel.

    We had a magnificent *view* from the top of the mountain.

flour, flower

> How much *flour* shall I use for the biscuit?
>
> Some men always wear a *flower* in their buttonholes.

frayed, freight

> The collar was too badly *frayed* to wear again.
>
> The furniture was shipped by *freight*.

fret, friend

> Did you hear the baby *fret* last night?
>
> A *friend* in need is a friend in deed.

guessed, guest

> I *guessed* the answer to the riddle the first time.
>
> Who is to be our *guest* for the week-end?

ice, eyes

> The *ice* on the pond was a foot thick.
>
> Her *eyes* are as blue as the skies.

lash, latch

> The sailors had to *lash* everything to the deck of the ship.
>
> I put the *latch* on the door when I came out.

lift, lived
> Do you think the fog will *lift* before noon?
> How long have you *lived* in the City?

loose, lose
> Everything in the house is at *loose* ends.
> Did anyone here *lose* an umbrella?

---

209. How Many

How many boys have joined the club?
" " " signed up for the trip?
" " " ever played bridge before?
" " has he brought home for dinner?
" " " she invited to the house?
" " " he interviewed for the position?
" " had we better ask for the week-end?
" " " subscribed for seats at the opera?
" " " been told of the plans for the summer?
" " am I to expect for the afternoon?

How many boys am I to vote for?
"   "   "   I to see this afternoon?
"   "   books is the box supposed to hold?
"   "   rooms " the house to have?
"   "   people " she supposed to call upon?
"   "   are at the football game?
"   "   " playing bridge?
"   "   " on the golf course?
"   "   were on the train?
"   "   " at church this morning?
"   "   " in the front row at the theatre?
"   "   will see the boxing bout?
"   "   " go to the Country Club with us?
"   "   " want rooms at the hotel?
"   "   would like some ice cream?
"   "   "   come if they were invited?
"   "   "   fly if they had the opportunity?
"   "   shall we invite for luncheon?
"   "   "   I speak to about the sightseeing trip?
"   "   "   I see about buying tickets?
"   "   seats should we reserve at the theatre?

COLLOQUIAL FORMS

How many should we serve at one time?
" " " I invite to the house party?
" " do you think will come?
" " " they expect for the conference?
" " women do their own housework nowadays?
" " does the automobile hold?
" " " the stadium seat?
" " " the theatre seat?
" " spoons did you find were missing?
" " " he tell you were going in one bus?
" " " the lecturer have in his audience?
" " books may I take from the library?
" " " I have today?
" " " we take with us?
" " might I interview at the office?
" " " we expect for the church supper?
" " can we invite for the Holiday?
" " " go in the boat at one time?
" " " the hotel accommodate?
" " could operate the radio set?
" " " take part in the game?
" " " solve the cross word puzzle?
" " games must be provided for the children?

How many people must be seen this morning?
"   "   pictures ought there to be in this package?
"   "   lamps ought we to have in the room?
"   "   newspapers do you read every day?
"   "   miles do you travel in a week?
"   "   automobiles have you?
"   "   play golf, bridge, tennis, football, baseball, etc.?
"   "   apple trees are in the orchard?
"   "   houses are on this street?
"   "   snowstorms did we have last winter?

210. Vowel Exercise

thew	thin	thee	tooth	kith	teeth
——	thug	then	——	doth	death
thaw	thar	that	north	hearth	hath

zoo	sit	seat	ooze	is	ease
sook	sun	set	puss	us	guess
saw	sard	sat	awes	cars	as

	rue	rid	reed
	rook	run	red
	raw	rah	rat

COLLOQUIAL FORMS

211. Homophenous Words

mention, pension

> Did you see any *mention* of the play in the paper?
>
> The soldier was given a small *pension*.

neck, deck

> The giraffe has a long *neck* and a small brain.
>
> We sat on *deck* until bedtime.

next, text

> Who lives in the *next* house?
>
> Do you remember the *text* of the sermon?

prove, proof

> It was hard to *prove* the truth of the statement.
>
> Who is to read the *proof* of the book?

refuse, reviews

> I had to *refuse* the invitation to the party.
>
> Who writes the book *reviews* for the newspapers?

rob, romp

> When did the thieves *rob* the bank?
>
> I like to watch the children *romp* in the Park.

safe, save
> You have my best wishes for a *safe* journey.
> You should *save* your strength for another day.

smell, spell
> The *smell* of food cooking made me hungry.
> Will you *spell* your name for me?

son, sun
> The *son* carried on his father's business.
> The *sun* has been shining all day.

steam, steep
> It is cold enough for *steam* heat.
> The road led up a *steep* hill.

---

212.   How Soon

How soon have you planned to leave for home?
"   "   "   you planned to visit us?
"   "   has the photographer promised the pictures?
"   "   "   the expressman promised to come for the trunk?
"   "   am I to start for California?
"   "   "   I due in Chicago?

COLLOQUIAL FORMS 201

How soon am I to hear from you?
"   "   is he to give his answer?
"   "   " there another train for Washington (Boston, Chicago, etc.)
"   "   " your son to leave for college?
"   "   are we to cross the equator?
"   "   " we to have our vacation?
"   "   " the lights to be turned off?
"   "   was I to wire you after I arrived?
"   "   " he told to come home?
"   "   " she to return the costume?
"   "   were we to let you have a reply?
"   "   " the films to be developed?
"   "   " the fires put out?
"   "   will the world come to an end?
"   "   " you write to me?
"   "   " everyone own an airplane?
"   "   would you call them on the phone?
"   "   " you like to have lunch?
"   "   " you like to have a swim?
"   "   shall we start for the theatre?
"   "   " we apply for passports?
"   "   " I begin the lesson?
"   "   should I send the check to the bank?
"   "   " I return the library book?
"   "   " we pass the Statue of Liberty?

How soon do the schools close for the summer vacation?
" " " the shops open in the morning?
" " " you want supper?
" " does the postman come?
" " " the moon rise?
" " " the sun set?
" " did he learn his way about the City?
" " " he tell us to return?
" " " the party reach the foot of the mountain?
" " may I expect you home?
" " " we have the car?
" " " we close the house for the summer?
" " might I call for you in the morning?
" " " I expect your reply?
" " " we hope to see you again?
" " can we walk on the fresh paint?
" " " you memorize the music?
" " " you be ready for us?
" " could the bridge be opened to traffic?
" " " you get ready to leave for the country?
" " " you be ready for lunch?
" " must I begin the work?
" " " we finish the course of lessons?

How soon must you leave us?
" " ought we to return the call?
" " " the party to arrive?
" " " we to publish the book?
" " do the leaves change color?
" " will the boat be in?
" " strange places become familiar.
" " it gets dark now.
" " will it stop raining?
" " should we turn on the lights?

213.   VOWEL EXERCISE

    wooed wit weed
    wood   won wet
    wart   what whack

choose	chin	cheat	hooch	hitch	each
should	shun	shed	push	hush	edge
short	shard	shad	torch	harsh	ash

214.   HOMOPHENOUS WORDS

arm, harm, harp

    I carried the books in my *arm*.
    No *harm* will come to you here.
    Who plays the *harp* in the orchestra?

bar, mar, par

> The boat was stuck on the sand *bar*.
> Water will not *mar* a good spar varnish.
> The stock is selling at *par*.

bark, mark, park

> Please open the door if you hear the dog *bark*.
> My fingers left a *mark* on the paint.
> Everyone seemed to be in the *Park* today.

bass, mass, pass

> We fished for *bass* in the lake.
> There is a *mass* of shrubbery around the house.
> Did you ever travel on a *pass*?

blaze, place, plays

> The fire will *blaze* up in a few minutes.
> You should have a *place* for everything and keep everything in its place.
> Who *plays* the organ at church?

bough, bow, mow

> The wind broke a *bough* from the pine tree.
> I thought I saw someone *bow* to me as I passed the house.
> The children are playing in the hay *mow*.

COLLOQUIAL FORMS 205

bundle, muddle, puddle

We sent a *bundle* of clothing to the Salvation Army.

How did things get into such a *muddle*?

I walked right into that mud *puddle*.

---

215. How Hard

How hard have you tried to learn French?
" " " you exercised this morning?
" " " the boys worked today?
" " has it rained here?
" " " your lesson been today?
" " " it been to find work?
" " had they worked for the play?
" " " she tried to reach me by phone?
" " " they tried before they succeeded?
" " am I to tie this knot?
" " " I to try to win the championship?
" " " I supposed to work?
" " is your egg boiled?
" " " the ice cream frozen?
" " " it snowing?
" " are the questions in the examination?
" " " the minister's lips to read?

How hard are we to study lip-reading?
" " was the wind blowing when you came in?
" " " it to understand me over the telephone?
" " " he working for his Master's degree?
" " were you thinking when I came in?
" " " you working last night?
" " " the words in today's lesson?
" " will they work for nothing?
" " " you study your lesson?
" " " he try for first place in the race?
" " would you work for five dollars?
" " " you work if you were given that position?
" " shall I make the frosting on the cake?
" " " I try to win first prize?
" " " I beat the eggs?
" " should the candy be?
" " " I try to find work?
" " " I work in the house?
" " do you study your lesson?

COLLOQUIAL FORMS 207

How hard do you think it will rain?
" " " you try to hide your real feelings?
" " does he cram for examinations?
" " " lip-reading seem to you?
" " " the water seem to be?
" " did you cry over the book?
" " " you try to get home in time?
" " " you find it to drive through the traffic?
" " must I push the door to open it?
" " " I hit the golf ball?
" " " we shove our way through the crowd?
" " ought the tire to be inflated?
" " " I to strike the blow?
" " " I to work to learn a trade?
" " the wind blows!
" " it rains!
" " it is to learn the truth sometimes.
" " we worked to get here on time.
" " this chair is!
" " the children have played today.

216.   Consonant Exercise

back	fag	whack	am	have	has
fag	whack	rack	have	has	hash
whack	rack	sack	has	hash	hath
rack	sack	shack	hash	hath	Hal
sack	shack	thank	hath	Hal	hat
shack	thank	lack			
thank	lack	tack			

217.   Homophenous Words

cheat, sheet, sheen

> Do many students *cheat* in examinations?
> We used a *sheet* for the moving picture screen.
> The silk has a beautiful *sheen*.

chop, job, shop

> We had to *chop* all the wood for the kitchen fire.
> The tramp was not looking for a *job*.
> There is a gift *shop* on almost every block.

dime, time, type

> The fare on the bus is a *dime*.
> It is *time* to go home for the day.
> That boy is an interesting *type*.

COLLOQUIAL FORMS

drag, drank, track

> We had to fairly *drag* the children away from the party.
>
> We made a cup of our hands and *drank* from the spring.
>
> It is almost impossible to keep *track* of the days of the month.

drip, trim, trip

> I could hear the *drip* of water from the faucet.
>
> The maid looks *trim* in her new uniform.
>
> The *trip* took us through beautiful country.

face, phase, vase

> Your *face* is very familiar to me.
>
> That is a new *phase* of the work.
>
> Where can I find a *vase* for the flowers?

limb, lip, limp

> A *limb* of the tree fell across the road.
>
> The baby cut his *lip* when he fell.
>
> The book is bound in *limp* leather.

218. Review of How Long, How Much, How Far, How Many, How Soon, How Hard

How long have you been away?
" far did you walk?
" much has been done on the work?
" many did you have?
" soon are you going away?
" hard must you work?

" many ought I to take with me?
" hard shall I study?
" long may I stay?
" much should I do?
" soon were you going?
" far will you walk?

" much does the house cost?
" soon will he come home?
" hard can I work?
" far are we going?
" many might I take?
" long would you stay?

" hard was he told to work?
" long will he stay?
" far will you go?

How much shall I take?
" soon can you be ready?
" many must you take?

" soon will you be back?
" much should I do?
" far ought I to walk?
" many might I have?
" hard did it rain?
" long could you stay?

" far do you want to walk?
" long can you stay?
" much have you with you?
" soon can you start?
" hard should I try?
" many ought I to take?

219.   CONSONANT EXERCISE

bard	far	what	arm	carve	cars
far	what	rah	carve	cars	harsh
what	rah	sard	cars	harsh	hearth
rah	sard	shard	harsh	hearth	Carl
sard	shard	thar	hearth	Carl	cart
shard	thar	lard			
thar	tart	lard			

220.   Homophenous Words

mice, buys, pies
>The barn is full of *mice*.
>Who *buys* the supplies for the house?
>There were mince and pumpkin *pies* for Thanksgiving.

plum, plumb, plump
>We make *plum* jelly every summer.
>That wall is not quite *plumb*.
>You should *plump* up the pillows every morning.

sad, sand, sat
>Why does everyone seem so *sad* today?
>The *sand* storm almost blinded us.
>We *sat* in the front row of the orchestra.

snake, stake, steak
>A black *snake* ran across our path.
>We fastened the boat to a *stake* on the beach.
>Do you prefer your *steak* rare or well done?

snub, stub, stump
>Why did that woman try to *snub* us?
>Do you like to write with a *stub* pen?
>Have you ever made a *stump* speech?

COLLOQUIAL FORMS

suck, sung, sunk

    The baby should not *suck* his thumb.

    The choir has already *sung* the anthem.

    The boat was *sunk* in the middle of the river.

swab, swamp, swap

    The doctor will *swab* out your throat for you.

    We found the flowers on the edge of the *swamp*.

    Small boys like to *swap* their possessions.

---

221.   WHAT

What have you ordered for breakfast?
" " you done with your pocketbook?
" " the men been doing all day?
" has been packed in the trunk?
" " been offered for sale?
" " been chosen for the prize?
" had caused the explosion?
" " we better do now?
" " been given out to the newspapers about the accident?
" am I to say when I see him?
" " I to report to headquarters?
" " I to expect from my family?

What is the plan for the day?
" " your favorite sport?
" " the matter?
" are your plans for the summer?
" " the colors of the rainbow?
" " you going to do this evening?
" was the cause of the fire?
" " the trouble with the radio?
" " the use of doing that?
" were your reasons for leaving the meeting?
" " you about to say to me?
" " they asking for their house?
" will the weather be like tomorrow?
" " I need for the journey?
" " you do if it rains?
" would you like for tea?
" " it cost to paint the house?
" " " cost to keep an automobile?
" shall I wear to the party?
" " I talk about to the class?
" " I charge on the account?
" should I put on the Christmas tree?
" " I say in my speech?
" " a boy of twelve weigh?
" do they think of the new house?
" " you think is right?
" " they ask for the property?

COLLOQUIAL FORMS 215

What does she do for a living?
" " the newspaper say this morning?
" " the doctor advise you to do?
" did he do with the flowers?
" " you do with the newspaper?
" " they make on the sale of bonds?
" time may we expect you home?
" " I do for you?
" " I read to you?
" can I say that will help you?
" " we do with the money?
" " you see from the window?
" could you expect under the circumstances?
" " he do for a sore throat?
" " I send as a wedding present?
" must be done at once?
" " we order from the grocery?
" " we save out of our income?
" ought we to say in the telegram?
" " to be done to relieve the situation?
" " we to talk about?
" time is it?
" picture is this?
" newspaper do you read?
" club do you belong to?
" is the price of gasoline?
" is the best you can do?

222. Consonant Exercise

paw	for	war	orb	cough	awes
for	war	raw	cough	awes	torch
war	raw	saw	awes	torch	north
raw	saw	short	torch	north	all
saw	short	thaw	north	all	awed
short	thaw	law			
thaw	law	daw			

223. Homophenous Words

aid, ate, eight, hate

>Have you taken a course in First *Aid* to the Injured?
>We *ate* all of our meals at the restaurant.
>The doors were opened at *eight* o'clock.
>War always breeds *hate.*

barge, marsh, parch, march

>The coal *barge* was in the way of the ferry boat.
>We found pink and white *marsh* mallows in the field.
>This sun will *parch* all of the lawns.
>The children *march* out of school in perfect order.

COLLOQUIAL FORMS 217

boarder, porter, border, mortar
> I am a *boarder* at the farm house.
> The *porter* will carry our bags to the train.
> I planted a *border* around the flower bed.
> There is not enough *mortar* between the bricks.

boast, most, post, posed
> The inventor is too modest to *boast* about his work.
> The guest did *most* of the talking.
> Will you *post* my letter for me?
> Who *posed* for the picture on the magazine cover?

bond, pod, pot, pond
> All college graduates are not *bond* salesmen.
> The seed *pod* should be picked before it opens.
> Is there any more coffee in the *pot?*
> There is a bowl of *pond* lilies on the centre table.

---

224.   WHY

Why have all the servants left?
"   " the stores closed for the day?
"   " prices gone up?

Why has the front door been left open?
"   "   the subway stopped running?
"   "   it turned so cold?
"   had the water supply given out?
"   "   the men stopped work?
"   "   you left the house before I came?
"   am I too late?
"   "   I asked to make a speech?
"   "   I so sleepy?
"   is he in such a hurry?
"   "   the train so late?
"   "   the light so dim?
"   are the roads so rough?
"   "   the workmen all standing around?
"   "   the streets in this part of town not paved?
"   was the house left open?
"   "   it wrong to catch the fish?
"   "   the Park so full of people today?
"   were all of the lawns in town turning brown?
"   "   the houses on the block all alike?
"   "   the books not returned before?
"   will the children ask so many questions?
"   "   you need to take a trunk?
"   "   you do such unexpected things?

COLLOQUIAL FORMS

Why would she hesitate about taking the position?
" " you refuse to go if I went with you?
" " it be necessary to leave so early?
" should you not do as you please?
" " old customs be revived?
" " the stores refuse to open an account for me?
" do you look at me that way?
" " the birds go South in the winter?
" " the blue jays make such a noise?
" does the wind always blow in Chicago?
" " the weather stay so cold?
" " a rolling stone gather no moss?
" did the dog bark all night?
" " you skate on the pond alone?
" " the children have to stay after school?
" can owls see in the dark?
" " cats climb trees and not come down?
" " parrots talk?
" could only one automobile cross the bridge at a time?
" must you leave so soon?
" " the car be left in the garage?
" " I report to the office this morning?
" ought we to be well informed?

Why ought the weather to be cooler?
" " the store to be open?
" is the air so damp?
" do we hurry so?
" " boys like to make a noise?
" " so many women like to play bridge?
" has the street been closed?
" do the leaves change color in the fall?

225. Consonant Exercise

bet	fed	wet	ebb	deaf	guess
fed	wet	red	deaf	guess	edge
wet	red	set	guess	edge	death
red	set	shed	edge	death	ell
set	shed	then	death	ell	end
shed	then	let			
then	let	ten			

226. Homophenous Words

count, gown, gout, gowned

You should *count* your change before leaving the window.

She wore a black velvet evening *gown*.

He has *gout* in his right foot.

She was *gowned* in the latest fashion.

doubt, down, town, noun

>Is there any *doubt* about the boat sailing on time?
>We drove *down* to the post office for the mail.
>The *town* is at the foot of the mountain.
>Is that word a *noun* or a verb?

dumb, dump, tub, numb

>That man is always kind to *dumb* animals.
>You may *dump* the groceries on the back porch.
>The warm *tub* bath was refreshing.
>My hands are *numb* from the cold.

laid, lain, lane, late

>How many eggs have the hens *laid* today?
>She has *lain* down for her afternoon nap.
>We strolled along the country *lane* in the twilight.
>We were *late* for church this morning.

money, muddy, putty, bunny

>How much *money* is in the bank?
>The water was too *muddy* for a swim.
>The windows will have to have more *putty*.
>The white *bunny* was the pet of the family.

227. WHEN

When have the painters promised to begin work?
" " you time to write so many letters?
" " the rooms been cleaned?
" has he asked for a vacation?
" " she planned to give the house-warming?
" " the store promised to deliver the furniture?
" had he been to a ball game before?
" " he sent in his resignation?
" " the elevators been inspected?
" is the golf tournament to be held?
" " our tennis match coming off?
" " my watch coming home from the jeweler?
" are you going to the football game?
" " the guests to arrive?
" " the boys coming home from camp?
" was America discovered?
" " Abraham Lincoln shot?
" " the World War begun?
" were the trees cut down?
" " the windows washed last?
" " the roads repaired?

COLLOQUIAL FORMS

When will the apple trees be in bloom?
" " cities be less noisy?
" " the boat arrive at the dock?
" would you like to have lunch?
" " we find them at home?
" " you like to see my garden?
" shall I expect you?
" " we three meet again?
" " I call for you?
" should the order for supplies be given?
" " the house be painted?
" " the lights be turned on?
" do you want the money?
" " the cars stop running at night?
" " the traffic lights change?
" does the moon rise tonight?
" " the evening star appear?
" " the policeman have his lunch?
" did Washington cross the Delaware?
" " the mail come in?
" " you finish the book?
" may I go shopping with you?
" " we see you again?
" " I open the house in the country?
" can we have the piano tuned?
" " the radio be repaired?
" " the rugs be cleaned?

When could we visit the college?
" " we go to the Art Museum?
" " we hang the pictures?
" must the papers be finished?
" " we ship the automobile?
" " you leave town?
" ought the lawn to be mowed?
" " we to start the furnace fire?
" " the building to be completed?
" will it ever stop raining?
" can we watch a class in lip-reading?
" does school open in the fall?
" is the house open for inspection?
" will the apartment be vacated?
" do the trains run on Sunday?
" has the postman been here?
" can I expect a reply to my telegram?

228. Consonant Exercises

pun	fun	won	up	huff	us
fun	won	run	huff	us	hush
won	run	son	us	hush	doth
run	son	shun	hush	doth	hull
son	shun	thug	doth	hull	hut
shun	thug	lug			
thug	lug	tug			

229. Homophenous Words

nags, tacks, tanks, tax

> That woman *nags* her family all the time.
> The *tacks* in the stair carpet are loose.
> Fortunately the fire did not reach the oil *tanks*.
> It is time to pay the income *tax*.

rap, wrap, ram, ramp

> You will have to *rap* on the door again.
> I like to *wrap* up Christmas presents.
> We were careful not to *ram* the other boats at the wharf.
> The children like to run down the *ramp*.

raise, rays, raze, race

> We watched the soldiers *raise* the flag at the fort.
> The invalid placed his chair in the direct *rays* of the sun.
> The workmen will have to *raze* the old house.
> How many boats are entered for the *race?*

recite, reside, resign, resigned

> The children like to *recite* a piece at school.
> Where does the Mayor *reside?*
> Why did you *resign* from the club?
> She has never been *resigned* to staying at home.

wait, wade, wane, weight

> I shall *wait* for you in the lobby of the theatre.
> The children like to *wade* in the brook in the summer.
> The moon has just begun to *wane.*
> His *weight* is just right for his height.

---

230.   WHERE

Where have I seen you before?
" " all the chocolates gone?
" " you been this summer?
" has he put the theatre tickets?
" " he left the car?
" " he kept his boat this summer?
" had that child hurt himself?
" " the train left the tracks?
" " the lightning struck the house?

COLLOQUIAL FORMS

Where is the capital of your state?
"   " the post office?
"   " the nearest telephone booth?
"   are the seats at the theatre?
"   " we going to board this summer?
"   " you living now?
"   was he told to wait for me?
"   " the first electric light made?
"   " the first gold mine in the United States?
"   were you this afternoon?
"   " they when you saw them?
"   " the furs stored?
"   will this bus take us?
"   " we find a good restaurant?
"   " you drive today?
"   would you build the house?
"   " you like to spend Christmas?
"   " you hunt for Captain Kidd's treasure?
"   shall I go to buy the book?
"   " I meet you?
"   " we look for the lost pin?
"   should we spend the summer?
"   " we put our wraps?
"   " we look for the others?
"   do you expect to be tomorrow?

Where do all the old movie films go?
"   "   we go from here?
"   does the rainbow end?
"   "   this road go?
"   "   he have his lunch?
"   did you find the flowers?
"   "   he park the car?
"   "   you lose your purse?
"   may I change these gloves?
"   "   I read in peace?
"   "   we have a conference?
"   might I expect to find quiet?
"   "   they find good movies?
"   "   we draw the line?
"   can we get a porter?
"   "   we find wild flowers?
"   "   I make my reservations for the train?
"   could I get a book to read?
"   "   we spend a more delightful hour?
"   "   I buy a sure cure for the "blues"?
"   must I deposit the check?
"   "   I go for information?
"   "   we send the bill?
"   ought the deed to the house to be recorded?
"   "   we to be now?

Where ought the records to be kept?
" did you get that hat?
" can we buy our railroad tickets?
" is the Statue of Liberty?
" have you been?
" ignorance is bliss 'tis folly to be wise.
" is the public library?

231. Consonant Exercise

book	foot	wood	(hoŏp hoŏf*)
foot	wood	rook	puss push pull
wood	rook	sook	push pull put
rook	sook	shook	pull put book
sook	shook	look	
shook	look	took	

232. Homophenous Words

badge, batch, match, mash, patch

The policeman wore the *badge* on his coat.
The cook has made a *batch* of bread.
Have you a *match* in your pocket?
I have to *mash* all of the vegetables for the baby.
The sport suit has *patch* pockets.

* The vowel in this group is commonly long o͞o, but sometimes is heard as short ŏo.

boll, mole, pole, bowl, poll

> Have you ever seen a *boll* of cotton?
> The *mole* burrows under the front lawn.
> The telegraph *pole* was blown down in the storm.
> There is a *bowl* of red roses on the table.
> How many votes did the President *poll*?

bump, bomb, mum, pump, pup

> Did that truck *bump* our fender?
> The news was like a *bomb* thrown into our midst.
> *Mum* is the word!
> We have to *pump* our water from the well.
> The *pup* is always ready to play with me.

cane, gain, gained, gait, gate

> The man carried a gold headed *cane*.
> The invalid will *gain* faster in a warm climate.
> My watch has *gained* five minutes in a week.
> That man has a peculiar *gait*.
> The *gate* receipts for the ball game were better than usual.

233.   WHICH

Which house have you bought?
" dress " you decided to wear this afternoon?
" book " you read?
" boy has been chosen president of the class?
" toy " the baby played with?
" boat had the advantage in the race?
" child had the most initiative?
" airplane had the best chance to win?
" bus am I to take at the corner?
" way " I to go from here?
" car " I to drive to the station?
" mountain is the highest?
" man " the favorite of the public?
" store " the best for leather goods?
" apartment are you considering?
" place " we to look at this morning?
" picture " we to keep for a souvenir?
" paper was the best?
" scenery " the most beautiful?
" meeting " he asked to preside over?
" children were left behind?

Which boxes were we supposed to pack?
" flowers " cut for the vases?
" hour will suit you best?
" " you have?
" method " you study?
" trip would give you the greatest pleasure?
" work " you like to do first?
" trunk " you like to have sent home?
" room shall I prepare for the guests?
" hat " I wear with this dress?
" store " I go to for books?
" should be done first?
" " I give to the Salvation Army?
" " be saved for another time?
" do you like best?
" " you want for your birthday?
" " the others prefer?
" does the better work?
" " he think is the more attractive?
" " your mother want you to have?
" way did the airplane go?
" room " they use for the class?
" lamp " you tell me to take?
" umbrella may I borrow?
" bags " I check at the station?
" room " I have?

Which office can I use?
"   puppy   " I have for my own?
"   day   " you meet us for lunch?
"   picture could you use?
"   rule   " they change?
"   club   " I join?
"   documents must be destroyed?
"   records " be kept?
"   papers   " be written over?
"   apples ought to be eaten at once?
"   suggestion should be given a trial?
"   house do you live in?
"   furniture goes into this room?
"   automobile do you like best?
"   train do you take in the morning?

234.   CONSONANT EXERCISE

bee	fee	wee	heap	eve	ease
fee	wee	reed	eve	ease	each
wee	reed	seed	ease	each	teeth
reed	seed	sheet	each	teeth	eel
seed	sheet	thee	teeth	eel	eat
sheet	thee	lee			
thee	lee	tea			

235. Homophenous Words

dice, dies, dyes, ties, nice

> Do we play the game with *dice?*
> Every flower I plant *dies.*
> The manufacturer used very pure *dyes* in the silk.
> The home *ties* are very strong.
> Now, do you think that was *nice?*

duck, dug, tongue, tuck, tug

> We had to *duck* into a doorway out of the rain.
> The workmen have *dug* up the street in front of the house.
> We were served cold sliced *tongue* for lunch.
> Wait until I *tuck* the children into bed.
> The two classes had a *tug* of war.

earn, heard, hurt, herd, urn

> He will *earn* everything he makes!
> I *heard* a robin this morning in the Park.
> No one was seriously *hurt* in the accident.
> The farmer has a large *herd* of cows.
> Please put the coffee *urn* on the table.

COLLOQUIAL FORMS

knack, nag, tack, tank, tag

> She has a *knack* of arranging flowers well.
> We hired an old *nag* from the farmer to go driving.
> You must not *tack* any pictures on the walls.
> We filled the gasoline *tank* before we started.
> I could not find the price *tag* on the dress.

---

236. Who or Whom*

Who have you asked about the repairs?
" " you been to for advice?
" " you spoken to about the position?
" has half a dollar to lend me?
" " been left in charge of the office?
" " been invited for the week-end?
" had the highest average for the year?
" " been in the house last?
" " made the highest score?
" am I to room with?
" " I supposed to represent in the pageant?

* *Note: As these "forms" are professedly colloquial Mr. Nitchie used "who" with each of the auxiliary verbs. Of course, any teacher who wishes may substitute "whom" for "who" in any sentence where it is grammatically correct—E. H. N.*

Who am I to ask for at the office?
" is to be the next president?
" " in the other room?
" " the pilot of the plane?
" are the members of the football team?
" " on the committee?
" " in the house party?
" was the man at the window?
" " at the house last night?
" " asked to serve refreshments?
" were the people I just met?
" " our first parents?
" " you talking to just now?
" will conduct the orchestra?
" " teach the lesson?
" " make the dress?
" would you propose for the office of treas-
urer?
" " like fried chicken for dinner?
" " like to have a vacation?
" shall we invite for dinner?
" " I ask for at the bank?
" " we have on the committee?
" should be the one to tell the news?
" " make the first move?
" " arrange the flowers in church?
" do you want to ask to play bridge with
us?

COLLOQUIAL FORMS

Who do you think will do for that part?
" " those people think they are?
" does the boy look like?
" " the housework for the family?
" " he like for a companion?
" may I take to the automobile show?
" " I offer the ticket to?
" " we bring home with us?
" might have the information we want?
" " be counted on for help?
" " we hope to interest in the house?
" can guess the answer?
" " get away for the afternoon?
" " put the deal through?
" must assume the responsibility?
" " have invitations to the reception?
" " write the letters?
" is that?
" came in just now?
" opened the door for you?

237. CONSONANT EXERCISE

bit	fit	wit	hip	if	is
fit	wit	rit	if	is	itch
wit	rit	sit	is	itch	kith
rit	sit	chick	itch	kith	kill
sit	chick	thick	kith	kill	kit
chick	thick	lick			
thick	lick	tick			

238. Homophenous Words

led, lead, lend, lent, let

> The band *led* the parade up the avenue.
> The pipes in the cellar were made of *lead*.
> Will you *lend* your home for the Benefit?
> The pictures were *lent* for the exhibition.
> I saw a To *Let* sign on the house.

palate, palette, mallet, pallid, ballot

> The boy talks as if he had a cleft *palate*.
> The artist's *palette* was covered with bright colored paints.
> I broke the handle of the croquet *mallet*.
> The patient was *pallid* from his long illness.
> For whom did you cast your *ballot*?

shun, jut, shunt, shut, shunned

> We shall *shun* that road in the future.
> The sign should not *jut* out into the street.
> They had to *shunt* the train onto the side track.
> Be sure to *shut* the window before you leave.
> He imagined that he was being *shunned*.

COLLOQUIAL FORMS

straight, strain, strait, strayed, strained

    We went *straight* home from the theatre.

    I heard a beautiful *strain* of music come from the church.

    The boat has passed through the *Strait* of Gibraltar.

    The dog has *strayed* away from home.

    I *strained* the fruit juices through a bag.

---

239. Review of What, Why, When, Where, Which and Who or Whom

What have you done today?
Why were you so late?
Where did you go?
Who shall I go with?
Which will you take?
When were you going away?

Who was at home?
Why did you come home?
Where is the post office?
Which may I have?
What can I do?
When should I go?

Where are you going?
When can you come back?
Why will you stay away?
Which did you want?
What is to be done?
Who do you like best?

Why does he stay away?
What had he been doing?
Where must we go?
Who shall we see?
Which will you do?
When must I go?

Where has he been?
Who would go with us?
Which may I have?
When ought I to go?
What can you say about it?
Why does he refuse to go?

Which will you have?
Where were you going?
What did you say?
When can I see you?
Who did you see?
Why has he gone away?

240. CONSONANT EXERCISE

bow	vow	wow	house	couch	south
vow	wow	row	couch	south	howl
wow	row	sow	south	howl	hound
row	sow	chow			
sow	chow	thou			
chow	thou	loud			
thou	loud	town			

241. HOMOPHENOUS WORDS

back, bag, bank, bang, pack, pang

    We shall be *back* in a week.
    I carried only an overnight *bag* with me.
    Who is the President of the *bank?*
    I am sure I heard the front door *bang.*
    We must *pack* our trunks at once.
    I felt a *pang* of homesickness when I left the house.

banner, banter, manner, batter, matter, patter

    A huge *banner* is hung across the street.
    He did not mind his friend's *banter.*
    The lecturer has a pleasing platform *manner.*
    I must stir up some *batter* for the waffles.
    What is the *matter* with the place?
    The *patter* of rain on the roof puts me to sleep.

cent, said, send, scent, sent, set

> What can you buy for one *cent?*
> The paper *said* the weather would be fair today.
> Where shall I *send* your baggage?
> The *scent* from the rose garden came through the windows.
> I *sent* the money to you by wire.
> Where shall I *set* out the trees?

coat, code, cote, cone, goad, goat

> Shall I put on a dinner *coat* tonight?
> The message was sent in *code.*
> The children have a dove *cote* in the back yard.
> Where did you get the ice cream *cone?*
> The police tried to *goad* the prisoner into a confession.
> The *goat* was tied up by the roadside.

---

242. Auxiliary Verbs With All Pronouns

Have I ever met you before?
" you called the number?
" they started home yet?
" we enough gasoline for the trip?

COLLOQUIAL FORMS

Has he applied for the position?
" she ever been abroad?
" it been raining here?

Had I known it I would have gone home.
" you been to Paris before?
" he read the morning paper?
" she bobbed her hair when you saw her?
" it cleared when you left?
" they finished the examination?

Am I making you nervous?
" I in the way?
" I too early?
" I dressed properly for dinner?

Is she alone in the house?
" he president of the company?
" it too late to change my mind?

Are we on time?
" you a good bridge player?
" they still talking?

Was he at the office on time?
" she a kindergarten teacher?
" it just what you wanted?

Were you talking to me?
" they prepared to fill the orders?
" we supposed to be there early?

Will I have time to go home for lunch?
  " you pour tea for me?
  " she get to the train on time?
  " they ever get through talking?
  " it be clear tomorrow?
  " he drive us home?

Would he take a job like that?
  " it look well in this room?
  " they pass us by?
  " she tell us what to do?
  " I have time to change my dress before dinner?

Shall we sit by the fire?
  " he be asked to go with us?
  " they be included in the party?
  " I phone you tomorrow?

Should we serve tea or coffee?
  " he have spoken to them?
  " I look over the ground again?

Do you care to have me read aloud?
 " they always come late?
 " I look as if I had gained weight?

Did they deliver the telegram promptly?
  " you ever see such luck!
  " it look just right to you?
  " he pilot the plane?
  " she ask for information?

COLLOQUIAL FORMS

Does he look like his father?
" it always rain on Sunday?
" she have a permanent wave?

May I speak to you for just a minute?
" we join the party?
" he be allowed to speak?

Might I ask a question?
" we help you?

Can she play the organ?
" I do anything more for you?
" they beat that record?
" he swim across the lake?
" it be possible that the storm is over?
" we use the tennis court now?

243.   CONSONANT EXERCISE

bow	foe	woe	hope	hove	hoe
foe	woe	row	hove	hoe	hose
woe	row	sow	hoe	hose	coach
row	sow	show	hose	coach	loathe
sow	show	though	coach	loathe	hole
show	though	low	loathe	hole	toad
though	low	tow			

244. Homophenous Words

crate, crane, grain, grade, grate, great
> Should we *crate* the furniture before it is shipped?
> The snow was removed by means of a *crane*.
> The field of *grain* looked like waving gold.
> There is a watchman at the *grade* crossing.
> There is a cheerful fire in the *grate*.
> Abraham Lincoln was a *great* man.

done, dun, ton, none, nun, nut
> What have you *done* today?
> You will have to *dun* him for the rent.
> There is only one *ton* of coal left in the cellar.
> We came home *none* too soon.
> The *nun* has a very sweet face.
> That is a hard *nut* to crack!

drain, train, trade, drained, trained, trait
> The *drain* will carry off the water from the roof.
> It was interesting to follow the speaker's *train* of thought.
> The Christmas *trade* has been heavy this year.

He *drained* his cup to the last drop.
The horse has been well-*trained*.
The boy's ambition is his most pronounced *trait*.

fad, fan, van, fat, vat, fanned

How long do you think the *fad* will last?
Do you feel a draft from the electric *fan*?
The furniture has been packed in the moving *van*.
Did you ever see anyone so *fat*?
The silk was dipped into a *vat* of dye.
The wind *fanned* the flames dangerously.

---

245. Negative Contractions with All Pronouns

Haven't I seen you somewhere?
   "   you had enough sleep?
   "   they a beautiful automobile?
   "   our letters been mailed?
   "   we enough coal for the winter?

Hasn't it been warm today!
   "   she an automobile license for this state?
   "   he been notified to report in the morning?

248 LIP-READING

Hadn't I better ring off?
" they driven over the road before?
" we better go by airplane?
" it made any impression upon them?
" he better try other work?
" you ever heard the opera?

Isn't he active for his years!
" it where I put it?
" she a fine looking woman!

Aren't you unusually well this summer?
" they living on the farm?
" we gay!
" her clothes becoming!
" his stories well written!

Wasn't it too bad that the rain spoiled our fun?
" she pleased with the present?
" he looking well when you last saw him?
" our play a success?

Weren't you free to do as you pleased?
" they all skilled musicians?
" we to be there at five o'clock?
" her rooms attractive?
" his friends pleasant?
" your proofs any good?

COLLOQUIAL FORMS

Won't you promise never to do it again?
" she make any reduction in the price?
" he get into trouble about the broken lease?

Wouldn't it be better to go back now?
" you like to do something frivolous?
" she be surprised to see us?
" her teacher excuse her from the class?
" his place be kept for him?
" they rehearse the play?

Shan't I be able to drive fast over the road?
" we serve dinner now?
" she change places with me?
" they take the family along?

Shouldn't we make reservations early?
" he go away for a few weeks?
" they be able to dock the boat?
" I play golf?
" she have consulted us first?

Don't you agree with me?
" they like their new home?
" we leave before nine in the morning?

Doesn't it beat all!
" she set a rapid pace?
" he like roast beef?

Didn't I tell you so?
    "   it take a long time to drive downtown?
    "   she look lovely?
    "   they order dinner for us?
    "   you pass me on the street?
    "   we have a good time!

Mightn't I try that, too?
    "   it be the better way out?
    "   he open the window?
    "   we appeal to the Red Cross?

Can't you look out for yourself?
    "   I have an afternoon off?
    "   they come some other time?
    "   we make the sandwiches now?
    "   he mend the chair?
    "   she make an apple pie?

Couldn't I do that for you?
    "   he walk on snow shoes?
    "   they hear us talking?
    "   he afford to rent the house?
    "   we compromise?
    "   it be done better than that?

Mustn't we exceed the speed limit?
    "   she leave the house today?
    "   he go walking now?
    "   they help us with our lessons?
    "   it be told?

Oughtn't he to be told the news?
" we to make other arrangements?
" you to take a vacation?
" they to be told of the accident?
" it to be published soon?

246.   CONSONANT EXERCISE

bow	beau	pew	house	hose	use
vow	foe	few	couch	coach	huge
row	row	rue	south	loath	youth
sow	so	sue	town	tone	tune
thou	though	thew			
loud	load	lieu			
now	no	new			

247.   HOMOPHENOUS WORDS

gilt, guild, guilt, killed, kilt, gild

The *gilt* has worn off of the frame.
Have you seen the new Theatre *Guild* play?
The man's *guilt* showed in his face.
The dry weather has *killed* the flowers.
The Scotsman was dressed in his *kilt*.
Will you help me *gild* the frame for the mirror?

munch, much, mush, budge, bunch, punch
> He likes to *munch* an apple while he reads.
> We had too *much* time on our hands.
> The *mush* was fried to a golden brown.
> We could not *budge* the big rock in the road.
> Did you ever have to *punch* a time clock?
> We gathered a *bunch* of wild flowers.

rode, road, roan, rote, rowed, wrote
> We *rode* all day in the day coach.
> Which *road* shall we take going home?
> My father always rode a *roan* horse.
> Some people cannot learn anything by *rote*.
> We *rowed* across the river for supplies.
> He *wrote* the letter by hand.

white, whine, whined, wind, wide, wine
> The sky is full of fleecy *white* clouds.
> I do not like to hear a child *whine*.
> The dog *whined* all the time you were away.
> Do you always remember to *wind* your watch?
> There is a *wide* porch on the side of the house.
> Will you have a glass of *wine* with your dinner?

248. Auxiliary Verbs Contrasted with Negative Contractions

Have you been in the house?
Haven't " " " " "
Has he been here before?
Hasn't " " " "
Had she promised to come?
Hadn't " " " "
Is it raining now?
Isn't " " "
Are you almost ready to go?
Aren't " " " " "
Was the paper delivered this morning?
Wasn't " " " " "
Were the children happy at camp?
Weren't " " " " "
Will you be at home in the morning?
Won't " " " " " "
Would he go for a drive with us?
Wouldn't " " " " " "
Shall we take the bus home?
Shan't " " " "
Should we leave before the play is over?
Shouldn't " " " " " "
Do the workmen leave at five o'clock?
Don't " " " " "

Does the road go past your house?
Doesn't " " " " " "
Did you have a good time?
Didn't " " " " "
Might we leave a message with you?
Mightn't " " " " " "
Can you see the river from the house?
Can't " " " " " " "
Could he come over at once?
Couldn't " " " " "
Must the work be finished today?
Mustn't " " " " "
Ought the children to be allowed in the barn?
Oughtn't the children to be allowed in the barn?

249. CONSONANT EXERCISE

pie	fie	why	I'm	I've	eyes
fie	why	rye	I've	eyes	tithe
why	rye	sigh	eyes	tithe	isle
rye	sigh	shy	tithe	isle	tide
sigh	shy	thy			
shy	thy	lie			
thy	lie	tie			

250. Homophenous Words

blade, plain, plate, plaint, plane, planed, played
    The knife is as sharp as a razor *blade*.
    The dress was perfectly *plain*.
    How large is the *plate* glass window?
    I listened to the beggar's *plaint*.
    The air*plane* was flying very low.
    The door will have to be *planed* off.
    She *played* a very good game of bridge.

bob, mob, mop, pop, pomp, palm, balm
    When did you *bob* your hair?
    There is a *mob* of people on the street.
    The maid should *mop* the kitchen floor.
    The boys were playing with a *pop* gun.
    There was much *pomp* and ceremony at the reception.
    The fortune teller read my *palm* at the Fair.
    The kindness of my friends is like *balm* to me.

bound, bout, mound, pound, bowed, mount, pout
    The men are *bound* by their contract to stay with the company.
    We watched the boxing *bout* at the Club.
    The house was built on a high *mound*.

How much is butter a *pound?*
We *bowed* our heads at the service.
Will you *mount* the photograph for me?
She will *pout* if she cannot have her own way.

---

251.   Why with All Negative Contractions

Why haven't my groceries been delivered?
"   "   I received by bank statement?
"   "   they sent us any word?
" hasn't the clock been put forward?
"   "   she washed the dishes?
"   "   the law been enforced?
" hadn't you provided a spare tire?
"   "   he brought evening clothes with him?
"   "   the sign been put up?
" isn't she going to be married?
"   "   he improving more rapidly?
"   "   there more light in the room?
" wasn't a policeman at the corner?
"   "   the laundry called for?
"   "   the alarm clock wound?
" weren't we expected to join the party?
"   "   you met at the station?

COLLOQUIAL FORMS

Why weren't they more tactful?
" won't the children behave?
" " the ice cream get hard?
" " the cream whip?
" wouldn't he dance with me?
" " she enjoy a summer at camp?
" " the motor boat go?
" shan't we try our luck at fishing?
" " I play with fire if I want to?
" " they do as they please?
" shouldn't I drive through that street?
" " they inspect the factory?
" " we tell the family?
" don't you like music?
" " they show a little more interest?
" " chestnut trees thrive in the East?
" doesn't he come home?
" " she come to see us?
" " the steamship company refund money?
" didn't you close the windows before it rained?
" " we think of that ourselves?
" " you wax the floors?
" mightn't I have a sample of the goods?
" " we walk along the road?
" can't you leave him alone?

Why can't I telephone to you?
"   "   the wires be repaired?
"   couldn't she use her voice?
"   "   you begin all over again?
"   "   he call off the strike?
"   mustn't I speak out loud?
"   "   he ever come here again?
"   "   they have a part in the discussion?
"   oughtn't the play to be rehearsed?
"   "   she to wear green?
"   "   that man to be elected?

252.   Consonant Exercise

bay	fay	way	ape	cave	——
fay	way	ray	cave	haze	age
way	ray	say	haze	age	lathe
ray	say	shay	age	lathe	ale
say	shay	they	lathe	ale	aid
shay	they	lay			
they	lay	day			

253.   Homophenous Words

been, bin, pin, pit, bid, bit, pinned, mitt
   Where have you *been* all this time?
   The flour *bin* has just been filled.

COLLOQUIAL FORMS 259

Be sure to *pin* the check to the bill.
You should *pit* the cherries before cooking them.
How much did you *bid* for the table at the auction?
The dog *bit* my hand when I patted him.
We *pinned* our faith on him.
She wore an old-fashioned lace *mitt*.

bold, bolt, mold, molt, poled, polled, bowled, mould

That was a *bold* plan he offered.
Don't forget to *bolt* the door at night.
Everything will *mold* in this damp weather.
The bird will soon begin to *molt*.
We *poled* the boat up the stream.
Who *polled* the most votes for president?
The wax was poured into a *mould*.
We *bowled* for an hour before dinner.

dead, debt, dent, tend, den, ten, tent, net

All of the trees seem to be *dead*.
The *debt* will soon be paid off.
There is a bad *dent* in the fender of the car.
Who will *tend* the furnace this winter?
The bears were followed to their *den*.

It is now *ten* o'clock.

I slept in a *tent* all summer.

How much were the *net* proceeds of the sale?

---

254. Pronouns with Contractions

I'm thinking of going South.
" through for the day.
" as happy as the day is long.

I'll meet you on the 5:45 train.
" see the thing through.
" never speak to him again!

I'd just gone out when you came in.
" rather sit in the orchestra than in a box at the theatre.
" be ashamed of myself if I did that.

I've promised to meet her this evening.
" never heard of such a thing.
" lived here all my live.

He's a jolly good fellow.
" a born leader.
" an authority on the subject.

He'll graduate from college in June.
" always be grateful to you for that.
" be here any minute.

COLLOQUIAL FORMS 261

He'd make a good comedian.
   " have to sign a paper.
   " take a chance any day.

She's a dead game sport.
   " developed a lot of executive ability.
   " just the one for the place.

She'll never make that train.
   " measure up to our expectations.
   " sail on the Mauretania.

She'd do well if she would only try
   " look well in that hat.

We're anxious to go home for Christmas.
   " just in time for dinner.
   " almost there now.

We'll let you know tomorrow.
   " soon be with you.
   " have to try something else.

We'd spent the day sightseeing.
   " like you to lunch with us.
   " spent all our money before we knew it.

We've a few minutes left before train time.
   " come over to say good-bye.
   " lost all our money in the failure of the bank.

You're the right person for the job.
  "   on the wrong track.
  "   just the person I wanted to see.
You'll hear from me in the morning.
  "   meet a lot of interesting people.
  "   not regret your decision.
You'd better make an early start in the morning.
  "   enjoy that story.
  "   be sorry if you missed the music.
You've been away a long time.
  "   never looked so well in your life.
  "   plenty of time for a visit.
They're planning an air route around the world.
  "   coming here for supper.
  "   taking part in the concert.
They'll see the thing through.
  "   never tell anyone what you said.
  "   have to haul the car out of the ditch.
They'd rather play baseball than eat.
  "   signed the papers before we arrived.
  "   made a mint of money in stocks and bonds.
They've made a wise decision.
  "   taken charge of everything.
  "   shown good judgment.

COLLOQUIAL FORMS

255.   CONSONANT EXERCISE

buy	bay	boy	I'm	ape	——
fie	fay	void	knife	cave	coif
~~why~~	~~way~~	——	~~ice~~	~~ace~~	~~toys~~
rye	ray	Roy	tige	age	——
sigh	say	soy	lithe	lathe	——
shy	shay	joy	isle	ale	oil
thy	they	——			
lie	lay	loin			
tie	day	toy			

256.   HOMOPHENOUS WORDS

died, tied, tide, tight, dyed, tine, nine, dine, night, knight, dined

The wind seems to have *died* down.

The grape vines were *tied* to stakes.

I do not like to swim when the *tide* is going out.

Are you sure the boat is water-*tight?*

The dress was *dyed* a dark blue.

One *tine* of the fork was broken.

We shall leave the house at *nine* in the morning.

Will you *dine* with us tonight?

We had to spend the *night* on the road.
King Arthur was a *Knight* of the Round Table.
We *dined* away from home tonight.

bend, bent, mend, meant, penned, pent, bed, pen, bet, pet, men, met

The house is just around the *bend* in the road.
The trees *bent* before the wind.
The laundry will *mend* your clothes for you.
I never *meant* to hurt your feelings.
He *penned* a few lines home.
They have a *pent*-house apartment.
We went to *bed* very early last night.
What kind of *pen* do you like to use?
How much will you *bet* on the race?
The *pet* monkey was always up to tricks.
The room was full of *men*.
The committee *met* at my house last night.

LESSONS ON VARIATIONS OF FUNDAMENTAL MOVEMENTS AND UNACCENTED VOWELS

257. The movements in the following lessons are variations of the fundamental sound-movements, or are movements for unaccented vowels, and therefore they have not the same drill value as the fundamental movements on which the preceding lessons are based. For this reason the lessons are placed at the back of the book to be used at the teacher's discretion (or the student's). They are excellent for advanced work, as the Practise Words of the lessons on unaccented vowels contain words of more than one syllable, whereas all Practise Words of the preceding lessons are of one syllable only.

The home practise on these lessons should be the same as that on the Lessons on the Movements.

R, After Vowel, Usually Showing No Movement

258. An *r*, after a vowel and before a consonant, as in "farm," usually shows no movement.

259. Practise Words

arm[1]	barbed	orb	warm[3]
harm[1]	sharp[2]	form	warp[3]
harp[1]	charm[2]	fort	short
farm	shark	born	thorn

260. Sentences

1. Were you vaccinated on the *arm?* 2. It will not do any *harm* to try for the prize. 3. That man *harps* on one subject all the time. 4. The *farm* was abandoned and overgrown with thorns. 5. Did you ever climb through a *barbed* wire fence? 6. There is a *sharp* wind from the Northeast. 7. What are you wearing for a watch *charm?* 8. A *shark* swam along in the wake of the ship. 9. The moon is the *orb* of night. 10. Your lips *form* the words very well. 11. The children made a snow *fort* in the yard. 12. The baby was *born* on board

ship. 13. It is *warm* enough to go without a coat. 14. The wood was badly *warped* from the dampness. 15. I have been reading a book of *short* stories. 16. Every rose has its *thorn*.

R, After Vowel, Relaxed–Medium

261. A final *r* in an unaccented syllable, occurring after a long vowel, tends to become like a short ŭ and to show the relaxed-medium movement; though it may show a slight puckered-corners.

262. *Practise Words*

fear	rear	deer[3]	sure
peer[1]	shear[2]	dear[3]	tour
beer[1]	cheer[2]	poor[4]	pure
we're	spear	moor[4]	cure

263. *Sentences*.

1. We will show neither *fear* nor favor. 2. I thought I saw you *peer* in at the window. 3. The workmen like *beer* with their lunch. 4. *We're* going away for a long time. 5. You will find a seat in the *rear* of the car. 6. When will the farmer *shear* the sheep? 7. *Cheer* up!

the best is yet to come. 8. Did you ever try to *spear* eels through the ice? 9. There are *deer* in the woods around the camp. 10. A baby is *dear* to its mother's heart. 11. The man was as *poor* as a church mouse. 12. The captain had to *moor* the ship in the Bay. 13. You must be *sure* to tell me about everything. 14. Would you like to take a *tour* around the world? 15. The water from the spring is as clear and *pure* as crystal. 16. Do you know anything that will *cure* a cold?

R, After Diphthong, Relaxed–Medium

264.   *Practise Words*

fire	ore	wore	door[2]
mire	four	roar	tore[2]
wire	pour[1]	sore	core
lyre	bore[1]	shore	hour
tire	more[1]	lore	sour

265.   *Sentences*

1. We can build a *fire* in the fireplace in a few minutes. 2. The truck was stuck in the *mire* on the side of the road. 3. I will *wire* you

as soon as I arrive. 4. I saw a gold *lyre* at the Museum of Art. 5. We had to change a *tire* on the way home. 6. How much *ore* has been mined this week? 7. I will meet you at *four* o'clock. 8. Will you *pour* the coffee while I pass the sandwiches? 9. I do not want to *bore* you with my story. 10. The *more* we know the more we want to know. 11. His enthusiasm *wore* off after awhile. 12. The surf broke on the beach with a *roar*. 13. I hope you are not going to have a *sore* throat. 14. Please shove the boat off from the *shore* for me. 15. Do you know the *lore* of the birds? 16. Will you please open the *door* for me? 17. I *tore* the letter into small pieces. 18. You must *core* the apples before you bake them. 19. At what *hour* shall I come to see you? 20. The milk will *sour* unless you keep it on ice.

Ur—Puckered–Corners

266. The sound of *ur,* as in "turn," shows usually only the puckered-corners movements; the *u* does not show a separate movement, but is absorbed by the *r*.

267. *Practise Words*

f*ur*	w*ere*	chi*r*p	c*ur*ve
fi*r*m [1]	whi*r*	lea*r*n	y*ear*ned
ve*r*b [1]	w*or*m	t*ur*n [2]	h*ur*t [3]
b*ur*rs	s*ur*f	di*r*t [2]	h*ear*d [3]

268. *Sentences*

1. It is too warm today for a *fur* coat. 2. May I speak to some member of the *firm?* 3. The foreigner used the wrong *verb* in his sentence. 4. The frost breaks open the chestnut *burrs.* 5. We *were* all home for Thanksgiving. 6. I could hear the *whir* of the machinery at the factory. 7. The early bird catches the *worm.* 8. Let's go swimming in the *surf.* 9. The birds *chirp* happily among the trees. 10. Some lessons are hard to *learn.* 11. At some street corners there is no left *turn,* and at others no turn at all. 12. The *dirt* road was rough and dusty. 13. The train came around the *curve* very slowly. 14. We *yearned* for the comforts of home. 15. Did you *hurt* yourself very much? 16. I *heard* a wonderful symphony concert last night.

Short ŏ

269. For the sound of short ŏ, as in "odd," "on," etc., there are two possibilities, depending upon the speaker's pronunciation.

First.—Short ŏ is more commonly heard as an extreme short sound of Italian *a* (ah); when so pronounced it shows the relaxed-wide.

Second.—Short ŏ is also quite commonly heard as an extreme short sound of broad *a* (aw); when so pronounced it shows the puckered-wide movement. A few words, such as "dog," "long," "lost," etc., are almost always heard with this sound.

270.   *Practise Words*

fob	shop[1]	odd[2]	long
pot	chop[1]	hot[2]	lost
what	dot	off	dog
rob	lot	soft	cross
sob	cot	loft	cost

271.   *Sentences*

1. Would you like a watch *fob* for Christmas? 2. A watched *pot* never boils. 3. *What* have you been doing today? 4. The boys

should not *rob* the bird's nest. 5. I could hear the baby *sob* as if his heart would break. 6. I had to *shop* around for a suit. 7. Did you have a *chop* for breakfast? 8. You must not forget to *dot* your i's and cross your t's. 9. The house is built on a one-hundred foot *lot*. 10. I slept on a *cot* all the time I was in camp. 11. What an *odd* name that man has! 12. There was a *hot* fire in the grate. 13. I am going *off* for an all-day tramp. 14. The turf was *soft* after the long rain. 15. The children had a happy time in the hay *loft*. 16. That is the *long* and short of the whole matter. 17. I thought you were *lost*. 18. The *dog* likes to ride on the front seat of the automobile. 19. You should not *cross* the street until the traffic lights change. 20. What would it *cost* to paint the house?

Long or *Short* oo

272. There are a number of words, such as "roof," that are currently pronounced with either the long or the short sound of *oo,* and hence show either the puckered-narrow or the puckered-medium movement. The long sound is more common.

LESSONS ON VARIATIONS

273. *Practise Words*

rōof	soon	hoofs
room	soot	hoop
root		

274. *Sentences*

1. The red tile *roof* of the house can be seen through the trees. 2. There is a homelike atmosphere about the *room*. 3. That is the *root* of the whole trouble. 4. I will be with you very *soon*. 5. The chimney was fairly choked with *soot*. 6. I saw the imprint of a deer's *hoofs* in the woods. 7. The little girl was rolling a *hoop* along the walk.

A in Path

275. There are a number of words, such as "path," in which the *a* commonly has the short sound, as in "pat," and the extended-wide movement, though a somewhat broader sound, nearly equivalent to *ah,* showing the relaxed-wide movement, is more correct.

276.   *Practise Words*

fast[1]	path[2]	blast	ask
vast[1]	bath[2]	class[3]	task
past	last	glass[3]	grasp

277.   *Sentences*

1. The snow is melting very *fast*. 2. There are *vast* forests in the Northwest. 3. We were traveling all the *past* month. 4. There are stepping stones in the *path* by the brook. 5. There is a bird *bath* in the garden. 6. Where were you *last* night? 7. The house shook from the *blast*. 8. All of the children in the *class* were promoted. 9. Would you like a *glass* of water? 10. Will you *ask* for my mail at the Post Office? 11. When you have finished your *task* you can rest for awhile. 12. A drowning man *grasps* at a straw.

X

278. The letter *x* represents a combination of two sounds, namely, of *k* and *s* (as "box" = "boks"), or of *g* and *z* (as "exact" = "egzact"). Hence, theoretically, the sounds represented by *x* show a combination of the throat movement and the tremor-at-corners, or extended-narrow movement; practically, however, the throat movement is seldom seen, so that *x* looks like *s* or *z*. This will be seen by contrasting "next" and "nest," "hoax," and "hoes."

279.   *Practise Words*

| fo*x* | fla*x* | ne*x*t[1] | mi*x* |
| bo*x* | si*x* | te*x*t[1] | phlo*x* |

280.   *Sentences*

1. Did you ever go on a *fox* hunt? 2. I bought a *box* of chocolate candy. 3. Her hair is the color of the *flax*. 4. The clock has just struck *six*. 5. I will see you again *next* week. 6. The workmen *mix* the concrete by machinery. 7. There is a large bed of hardy *phlox* in the garden.

Unaccented Vowels

281. Accented vowels are those occurring in syllables which are stressed or emphasized; unaccented vowels are those occurring in syllables which are not stressed. For example, in "after," the first syllable is stressed or accented, while the final syllable is unstressed or unaccented.

In ordinary, colloquial speech almost all unaccented vowels are spoken very carelessly, often slovenly. The result is that they usually show either the relaxed-medium or the relaxed-narrow movement. The relaxed-medium movement is more common, and any unaccented vowel may show it.

Many unemphatic words of one syllable have the effect of loss of accent when pronounced rapidly and naturally in sentences. Such words are particularly prepositions, as *to, of, on, by,* etc.; conjunctions, as *and, or;* the articles, *a, an, the;* and the auxiliary verbs, as *has, had, can,* etc.

Extended Movements, Tending, When Unaccented, to Become Relaxed

282. The accented and unaccented vowels occurring in this group may be represented by the words: r*ee*f, r*e*fer; f*ie*rce, f*e*rocious; g*e*t, targ*e*t; f*a*ce, surf*a*ce; tar*e,* elementary.

LESSONS ON VARIATIONS

283: *Practise Words*

be*f*ore	d*e*pend	sur*f*ace
be*l*ow	*e*rect	aver*a*ge
re*f*er	*e*ruption	yesterd*a*y
pre*f*er	*f*erocious	element*a*ry
re*m*ove	mark*e*t	rudiment*a*ry
re*w*ard	tar*g*et	ros*a*ry
se*v*ere	contente*d*	

284. *Sentences*

1. I am sure it will rain *before* long. 2. I went *below* when the weather was rough. 3. Can you *refer* me to a good summer hotel? 4. I *prefer* not to talk about the matter. 5. When will the workmen *remove* the rubbish? 6. The *reward* of perservance is sure. 7. There was a *severe* wind storm last night. 8. I *depend* upon you to write me all the news. 9. Who is to *erect* the building at the corner? 10. The *eruption* of the volcano did not do any damage. 11. The lion looked very *ferocious*. 12. Are you going to *market* this morning? 13. The marksman hit the *target* in the bullseye. 14. She is perfectly *contented* with her lot in life. 15. The *surface* of the lake is frozen.

16. What is the *average* attendance at church?
17. I met your friend *yesterday* on the street.
18. He has only an *elementary* education. 19. He has only a *rudiamentary* knowledge of electricity. 20. She carried a *rosary* in her pocket.

Unaccented Relaxed Movements

285. The accented and unaccented vowels occurring in this group may be represented by the words: p*i*t, p*u*lp*i*t, d*i*re, d*i*rect.

286. *Practise Words*

*i*mpose	d*i*spose	hurr*y*	cheer*y*
*i*nfer	p*i*ano	worr*y*	g*i*gantic
*i*nsure	p*u*lp*i*t	wear*y*	d*i*rect
*i*llegible	splend*i*d	worm*y*	em*i*gration

287. *Sentences*

1. You should not allow anyone to *impose* on you. 2. What am I to *infer* from the reports? 3. Have you *insured* the house against fire? 4. His handwriting is so *illegible* I cannot make out what he is trying to say. 5. I am not *disposed* to contribute to the fund. 6. Did

I hear you playing on the *piano*? 7. Who occupied the *pulpit* at the church? 8. We had a *splendid* vacation in the mountains. 9. You will miss the train unless you *hurry*. 10. Don't *worry* about things that cannot be helped. 11. I am *weary* of hearing him talk about his troubles. 12. I think that is a *wormy* apple you have. 13. There is a *cheery* fire in the living room. 14. Some of the trees in California are *gigantic* in size. 15. Which is the most *direct* road to the town? 16. The *emigration* from Europe to America is very large.

Puckered Movements, Tending, When Unaccented to Become Relaxed

288. The accented and unaccented vowels occurring in this group may be represented by the words: t*oo*, t*o*day; acc*u*se, acc*u*sation; c*u*re, acc*u*rate; f*u*ll, awf*u*l; s*u*re, eras*u*re; *o*pe, *o*pinion; *o*re, *o*ration; *aw*e, *au*gust (adj.); *o*ff, *o*fficial; s*i*r, s*u*rprise. In rapid speech these unaccented vowels tend to become relaxed, though in more careful speech, they will show a slight puckering of the lips.

289. *Practise Words*

t*o*day	acc*u*rate	*o*pinion	f*o*rlorn
t*o*morrow	beautif*u*l	pr*o*pose	mirr*or*
s*u*perior	wonderf*u*l	vi*o*lin	rum*or*
st*u*pendous	delightf*u*l	h*o*rizon	riv*er*
acc*u*sation	pleas*u*re	a*u*thority	s*u*rprise
comm*u*tation	meas*u*re	*o*fficial	

290. *Sentences*

1. Are you going downtown *today?* 2. *Tomorrow* will be time enough for the work. 3. Means of transportation are much *superior* to those of a century ago. 4. There has been *stupendous* progress in all lines of invention. 5. I do not believe the *accusation* against him is true. 6. Have you bought your *commutation* ticket for next month? 7. He gave a very *accurate* report of what he saw. 8. The sunset last night was *beautiful*. 9. That opera singer has a *wonderful* voice. 10. The weather was most *delightful* all the time we were gone. 11. It will give me a great deal of *pleasure* to have you go with me. 12. Will you *measure* me and see how tall I am? 13. What is your *opinion* of the story? 14. I do not *propose* to allow him to have the book. 15. Do you play

the *violin?* 16. There was not a single ship on the *horizon.* 17. Who is your *authority* for the statement? 18. I have the *official* report of the association. 19. You look very *forlorn* this afternoon. 20. I have an old-fashioned *mirror* in the living room. 21. I heard a *rumor* that you were going to move West. 22. Will you row me across the *river?* 23. Were you very much *surprised* to find me here?

Unaccented Relaxed Movements

291. The accented and unaccented vowels occurring in this group may be represented by the words: *u*p, *u*pon; f*a*r, sof*a*; c*o*n, c*o*nvince.

292. *Practise Words*

*u*pon	preci*ous*	b*a*rometer
*u*ntil	illustri*ous*	c*o*nfer
s*u*ppose	spontane*ous*	c*o*nfession
s*u*cceed	sof*a*	c*o*mmission
s*u*ggestion	dram*a*	*o*bjection
s*u*fficient	gorill*a*	*o*ppose
lusci*ous*	parad*e*	*o*ccur

293. *Sentences*

1. *Upon* my word, I never thought of that. 2. I will wait here *until* the sun goes down. 3. What do you *suppose* they will say when they hear the news? 4. If at first you don't *succeed*, try, try again. 5. Have you any *suggestions* to make for the party? 6. There will be *sufficient* time to finish everything. 7. That was a *luscious* peach I had for breakfast. 8. She lost two *precious* stones from her ring. 9. Longfellow was the most *illustrious* of our American poets. 10. The fire was caused by *spontaneous* combustion. 11. There is an old-fashioned *sofa* in the farmhouse parlor. 12. Are you particularly fond of the *drama?* 13. I saw a *gorilla* at the menagerie yesterday. 14. All the children ran to see the circus *parade.* 15. The *barometer* fell very low last night. 16. We must *confer* as to the best course to pursue. 17. An honest *confession* is good for the soul. 18. Have you any *commission* for me this morning? 19. Have you any *objection* to my going with you? 20. Is anyone *opposed* to the new rules? 21. I hope you will not let that *occur* again.

LESSONS ON VARIATIONS

Extended Movements, Tending, When Unaccented to Become Relaxed

294. The accented and unaccented vowels occurring in this group may be represented by the words: *a*ble, *a*bility; *a*dd, *a*dvance.

295. *Practise Words*

*a*bility	*fa*cility	*a*ffirm	workm*a*n
*a*bove	c*a*sino	*a*ppear	music*a*l
*a*bout	*a*dvance	*a*gain	dist*a*nt

296. *Sentences*

1. She has a great deal of literary *ability*. 2. Who has the apartment *above* yours? 3. I will meet you at the office at *about* twelve o'clock. 4. Have you any *facility* in the use of carpenter's tools? 5. I should like to have you go with me to the *casino* tonight. 6. How rapidly have you *advanced* in your work? 7. I will *affirm* the truth of the statement positively. 8. You *appear* to be having a good deal of trouble. 9. I will see you *again* in the morning. 10. The man who helped me was a very good *workman*. 11. Have you any *musi-*

cal talent? 12. How far is the moon *distant* from the earth?

Lost Unaccented Vowels

297. There are some words in which the unaccented vowel is either lost or so slightly pronounced as to show no movement, as "poison" becomes "pois'n."

298.   *Practise Words*

pois*o*n	pleas*a*nt	miss*io*n	nat*io*n
less*o*n	fast*e*n	oc*ea*n	leg*io*n

299.   *Sentences*

1. The bottle on the shelf was marked "*poison*." 2. I hope that will be a *lesson* to you. 3. We had very *pleasant* weather for the journey. 4. Will you help me *fasten* my skates on? 5. Have you seen the old Spanish *missions* of Southern California? 6. The *ocean* is as blue as sapphire today. 7. The whole *nation* was thrilled by the news. 8. He was an officer in the Foreign *Legion*.

COLLOQUIAL SENTENCES

300. These sentences are intended to be used in the same manner as all other sentence-material in the book. Many additional sentences will be suggested by those given. These sentences may be used as the basis of definite conversation practise, also.

301.   TIME

1. What time is it? 2. It is very late. 3. It is almost five o'clock. 4. I got up at seven this morning. 5. We will have lunch at twelve. 6. I am to meet you at three o'clock. 7. Your lesson is at eleven-thirty. 8. The store closes at five. 9. The trip took two days. 10. We have a three year lease on the house. 11. I shall be ready in five minutes. 12. We are going away for a month. 13. The train was an hour late. 14. The lesson will last forty-five minutes. 15. The boat is a day overdue. 16. We have fifteen minutes in which to catch the train. 17. I am going away for two weeks. 18. There are

seven days in the week. 19. Breakfast is served at seven-thirty. 20. What time did your friends arrive? 21. The bus runs every half hour. 22. The train runs every hour on the hour. 23. The bank closes at three o'clock. 24. The office opens at nine. 25. The letter was mailed late in the afternoon.

302. Traveling

1. How far it is to Philadelphia? (Boston, Chicago, San Francisco, etc.) 2. Did you make the trip by automobile? 3. We drove to Florida last winter. 4. When are you going abroad? 5. Which boat shall we take to California? 6. We took a trip last summer to Yellowstone Park. 7. We decided to fly to Washington. 8. We took a trip around the City in a sightseeing bus. 9. We drove all day through the mountains. 10. Shall we go to Mexico by boat? 11. We took a trip through the Great Lakes. 12. How long were you in England? 13. The trip around the world took six months. 14. We went from New York to Chicago by airplane. 15. We drove 300 miles in one day. 16. Have you ever been in Paris? 17. We met a party of friends in Egypt. 18.

Shall we go to Bermuda this winter? 19. We are going to Quebec for the winter sports. 20. We are planning a trip to South America. 21. How long will the cruise to South Africa last? 22. How much will the Mediterranean trip cost? 23. How would you like a trip to the Land of the Midnight Sun? 24. We took the boat to Jacksonville. 25. Have you seen Niagara Falls in the winter?

303.   ART

1. I suppose that the Venus de Milo is the most famous statue in the world. 2. Swedish glass is famous all over the world. 3. The most famous statue of George Washington is in Richmond, Va. 4. When you are in Washington be sure to see the great statue of Abraham Lincoln. 5. Sir Joshua Reynolds, the great English portrait painter, was deafened in early life. 6. Can you name two other famous painters who had an impairment of hearing? 7. Have you ever seen the picture called The Horse Fair by Rosa Bonheur? 8. The ruins of Pompeii have much to tell us about the art of the Romans. 9. A well-known American artist painted a portrait of his mother which

is now in the Louvre. 10. I found a lovely Wedgewood bowl in grandmother's china closet. 11. How many of the French cathedrals have you seen? 12. The Cathedral of Notre Dame in Paris was begun in 1163. 13. Who painted the "Blue Boy"? 14. I sometimes think that the Chinese are the most artistic people in the world. 15. Who would you say is America's greatest portrait painter? 16. Raphael was only thirty-seven years old when he died. 17. Was Michaelangelo greater as a painter or as a sculptor? 18. Rembrandt painted a great many portraits of old men and old women. 19. Have you ever visited the American Wing of the Metropolitan Museum of Art in New York? 20. "A thing of beauty is a joy forever."

304. Shopping

1. Do your Christmas shopping early. 2. Where shall I buy a winter coat? 3. We hunted all day for a coat we liked. 4. The stores were too crowded for comfort. 5. There was a private sale of dresses today at (give name of some local store). 6. Where is the notion department? 7. Please charge this to

COLLOQUIAL SENTENCES

my account. 8. Will you deliver the things today? 9. Where did you find the blankets? 10. The salesman showed me everything he had. 11. I just looked around the shops without buying anything. 12. Everything was too expensive for me. 13. I never saw things so cheap. 14. I like to go "window shopping." 15. Which store carries the best leather goods? 16. I must buy a wardrobe trunk before I go away again. 17. Where shall I buy gloves? 18. The table was covered with bargains. 19. The Lost and Found desk is on the first floor. 20. The house furnishings are on the fifth floor. 21. It is always a pleasure to shop in that store. 22. The Christmas displays were more fascinating than ever. 23. There is always a furniture sale in August. 24. January is a good time to buy linens. 25. Shopping is the most tiresome thing in the world!

305. RADIO

1. What kind of radio set have you? 2. Did you hear the concert last night? 3. The program was interrupted by an S. O. S. 4. The President's speech was heard over a nation-wide hookup. 5. Which announcer do you like

best? 6. We were thrilled by the football game as we listened to it over the radio. 7. Radio sets change in style almost over night. 8. Is there much demand for radio engineers? 9. The boarders are not allowed to turn on the radio. 10. There was too much static last night for us to hear the program. 11. Have you a lightning arrestor on your set? 12. Radio is one of the greatest contributions to present-day life. 13. We visited the Radio Room on the ship. 14. The radio industry has had a phenomenal growth. 15. Do you believe that sermons over the radio keep people from going to church? 16. The radio gives a great deal of pleasure to invalids and shut-ins. 17. Through the radio Admiral Byrd and his men were in constant touch with home. 18. The radio takes the best music into homes everywhere. 19. The radio has made travel by sea much safer than in the old days. 20 Every part of the world is constantly in touch with every other part. 21. Which station has the best programs? 22. We are in a "dead" zone for one of the largest stations. 23. The loud speaker has a beautiful tone. 24. The radio makes it possible for many deafened people to hear good music, lectures, etc. 25. What are the latest developments in the radio field?

306. BRIDGE

1. Do you play bridge? Let's make up a table for a game of bridge. 3. Do you observe all the conventions? 4. Shall we draw for partners? 5. Shall we pivot or progress? 6. I prefer to play rubbers. 7. Please shuffle the cards. 8. It's your deal first. 9. Who is the first bidder? 10. I'll bid two diamonds. 11. You will have to bid three if you want to make it diamonds. 12. I'll bid four clubs. 13. I'll double that bid of four clubs. 14. It's your deal next. 15. Did you take me out of my no trump bid? 16. We lost by one trick! 17. How many honors did you have? 18. There were two honors in the dummy. 19. What is the score? 20. Oh! dear, you trumped my ace. 21. Why didn't you return my original lead of spades? 22. My opponent had a singleton in hearts. 23. Hurrah! we made a grand slam. 24. Did you cut the cards? 25. We had simple honors.

307. AUTOMOBILES

1. What make of car have you? 2. When will the car be delivered? 3. The brakes

worked perfectly on the mountain. 4. It was hard to keep the car on the road in the storm. 5. The new car steers with just a touch of the wheel. 6. How many miles can you make on a gallon of gasoline? 7. We had a punctured tire on the way home. 8. Be sure to get water, oil and gasoline at the next stop. 9. What is the wheel-base of your new car? 10. You didn't shift gears quickly enough. 11. I didn't see the traffic light in time to stop. 12. We had to put on the chains before starting out. 13. The road test was very severe. 14. The car is upholstered in grey. 15. What will keep the windshield clear in freezing weather? 16. Be sure to leave the parking lights on. 17. You should dim your lights when passing another car. 18. We had to go down the hill in second. 19. The car should be washed before it is driven again. 20. When was the oil changed? 21. Were the springs greased? 22. That hill was too much for a new car. 23. The new sport model is a beauty. 24. Those tires have given service for ten thousand miles. 25. The windshield is unbreakable.

308.   FOOTBALL

1. Who is refereeing the football game today? 2. Who is playing at the Stadium? 3. How long are the quarters? 4. Will either team use the hidden-ball play? 5. Either team can resort to the forward pass in an emergency. 6. Has the "huddle" proved a success? 7. Will the quarter-back call signals? 8. How far is the average punt of the fullback on team A? 9. The delayed crossbuck is a good end play. 10. What is the penalty for off-side play? 11. In case of a fumble, does the team in possession of the ball lose it? 12. The forward pass is always a dangerous maneuver. 13. The lateral pass has come into play of late. 14. Drop-kicking is on the wane. 15. The goal posts are set ten yards in the rear of the goal lines. 16. First down ten to go. 17. Fourth down goal to go! 18. "Bone-crushing" tackling pleases the crowd. 19. "Hold 'em Yale!" 20. There is a thirty minutes intermission between the halves. 21. An off-tackle slash is generally good for a few yards. 22. The "Minnesota shift" in its day was very successful. 23. The snapper-back is a very hard position to play. 24. "Down the field!" 25. The game is ours!

309.   SCHOOL

1. Where do the children go to school? 2. Do you teach the fifth grade? 3. How many children are in the kindergarten? 4. The boy has gone away to preparatory school. 5. Who spoke at the Assembly today? 6. I had to stay for a Teachers' Meeting. 7. The children were very restless all morning. 8. When does your daughter enter high school? 9. The college entrance examinations are held in June. 10. Who is Superintendent of Schools? 11. The fire drill was held this morning. 12. Who is to have charge of the playground at noon? 13. Every child in the class was promoted. 14. Commencement Day is nearly always hot. 15. The Freshman class this year is larger than ever. 16. Is the student taking post-graduate work? 17. Who has the primary class? 18. The district school has been closed for the summer. 19. The children ride to school in a bus. 20. There is no high school in the town. 21. There is a seat for every child. 22. You will be late for school unless you hurry. 23. Who is your class teacher? 24. The principal visited each room. 25. The Parent-Teachers Association meets tonight.

310. GOLF

1. Keep your head down and your eyes on the ball. 2. The heavy rain has made the course very wet. 3. I drove a ball almost 300 yards straight down the fairway. 4. How many clubs do you carry in your bag? 5. Do you like a steel-shaft driver? 6. Do you play better with the wooden clubs or the irons? 7. For the last three days I have hooked my drive into that rough. 8. Your niblick is the club to use to get out of that sand trap. 9. This course is hard for me because it is so different from ours. 10. Do you prefer match or medal play? 11. What club shall I use for the water-hole? 12. The putting greens are in wonderful condition this season. 13. If your approach is perfect, the ball will drop dead. 14. Can you sink a ten foot putt? 15. There is a penalty for a lost ball. 16. My ball is lying in a hazard. 17. It is very easy to slice a brassie shot. 18. The ground is so wet that it is hard to get a good lie. 19. There will be a putting match this afternoon. 20. That ball is out of bounds. 21. My greatest ambition is to be a scratch player. 22. You will have to use your mashie to play out of the rough. 23. Have you ever played in a 36 hole

match? 24. I lost the match on the eighteenth green. 25. You will have to change your grip.

311. THE HOUSE

1. How many rooms are there in the house? 2. The bedrooms are all on the second floor. 3. There is a reading lamp by the easy chair. 4. You will find the magazines on the centre table. 5. You may put your coat and hat in the hall closet. 6. There is an open fire in the sitting room. 7. There are flowers in every room in the house during the summer. 8. The sun parlor is always warm and cheerful. 9. We serve lunch in the breakfast room. 10. The kitchen is bright and sunny. 11. The windows should be washed while the weather is good. 12. The maid should dust the furniture. 13. There were books and magazines everywhere. 14. The desk was covered with papers. 15. The house should be thoroughly aired before the family arrive. 16. Do you use a vacuum cleaner and other electrical appliances? 17. The electric refrigerator is a great comfort. 18. You will find the laundry in the basement. 19. There are four elevators in the hall. 20. The house is set back one hundred feet from

the street. 21. The lawn is always beautifully kept. 22. The house has a red tile roof. 23. The playroom is flooded with sunshine. 24. Where is the music room? 25. It is home to us!

312.   Music

1. I would rather hear good music than go to a play. 2. Are you musical? 3. Please play something for me on the piano (violin, 'cello, flute, etc.). 4. What do you think of jazz? 5. Some of our largest cities have their own symphony orchestras. 6. Have you ever watched the famous conductors lead an orchestra? 7. I get tired of hearing jazz on the radio. 8. The school orchestra gave a concert last night. 9. It is the dream of every great artist to perform with a symphony orchestra. 10. Some people go to the opera every week during the season. 11. No one who had heard Caruso could ever forget his wonderful voice. 12. I should like to hear all of Wagner's operas at Bayreuth. 13. Have you ever sat in the "diamond horseshoe" at the Metropolitan Opera House in New York? 14. When Kreisler gives a recital there is hardly standing room in the house. 15.

Knowledge of music is an education in itself. 16. It is interesting to compare the old masters with the works of modern composers. 17. Every college has a Glee Club. 18. The Negro singer has wonderful deep tones in his voice. 19. Do you prefer mixed voices or a choir of men and boys? 20. Many boys who become good singers get their start in a choir school. 21. The Negro spirituals and plantation melodies are America's only folk songs. 22. An Intercollegiate Glee Club concert is something really worthwhile. 23. The orchestra played Stravinsky's "Fire Bird" at the last concert. 24. No one who has ever heard them can forget Beethoven's symphonies. 25. "The New World Symphony" by Dvorak sends everyone home humming the lovely music.

313. VACATION

1. We spent our vacation at home this year. 2. October is an ideal month for vacation. 3. She has all summer off. 4. We expect to spend our vacation touring in the car. 5. It rained the two weeks we were away. 6. We lived at a farm house last summer. 7. I took my vacation in week-ends. 8. Shall we go to the sea-

shore this summer or to the mountains? 9. The children have four months vacation from school. 10. Our friends went for a trip to Alaska. 11. Everyone should have a vacation. 12. I am ready for mine! 13. We are going to the North Woods for a hunting trip. 14. We lived out of doors all summer. 15. We camped in the Rocky Mountains. 16. I took a canoe trip in Maine. 17. We spent a month cruising along the coast. 18. The boys tramped through England all summer. 19. He worked his way across the ocean. 20. The children spent two months at camp. 21. We went to Florida in January for a winter vacation. 22. The children came home from camp as brown as berries. 23. The men like nothing better than to go fishing. 24. We spent our days in exploring the woods. 25. We went on a cruise to South America.

314. WEATHER

1. What does the paper say about the weather? 2. We have had sunshine every day for a month. 3. How long does the rainy season last? 4. Those black clouds are only wind clouds. 5. How much snow fell last night? 6.

The thermometer is twenty below zero. 7. We had a "white" Christmas this year. 8. The weather is much too warm for this time of the year. 9. We are apt to remember only the unusual weather. 10. The August nights were delightfully cool. 11. This snow will make perfect coasting. 12. The thunder shower came up in a few minutes. 13. If it keeps on raining the rivers will soon overflow their banks. 14. The water in the reservoirs is very low. 15. Do you think it will rain before morning? 16. The summer heat in some parts of the country is unbearable. 17. We never pay any attention to the rain here. 18. The air is as balmy as spring. 19. Not a drop of rain fell for months. 20. Our climate is delightful all the year around. 21. A few days more of this cold weather and the skating will be perfect. 22. I have never before seen the fields so green in August. 23. Which way does the wind blow? 24. The weather was perfect while we were on the ocean. 25. The weatherman is more often right than wrong.

315. Books

1. Did you remember to take the books back to the Library? 2. The children's books of to-

day are fascinating. 3. The boys are fond of books of adventure. 4. It is impossible to keep up with the new books. 5. Where shall I find books of reference? 6. I sat up nearly all night to finish the book. 7. Nothing rests me so much as to read a good novel. 8. I found the book of travel most interesting. 9. The reference books are in another department. 10. So few people nowadays read the classics. 11. Which is the best seller this year? 12. How much does the Circulating Library charge a week? 13. You will have to have the book reserved. 14. A dictionary should be in every home. 15. Books help to make a real home. 16. The children were taught to read good books. 17. The book was reviewed in last Sunday's paper. 18. I like to browse among the books in the Library. 19. Who is your favorite author? 20. I read the book in a few hours. 21. May I borrow the book when you are through with it? 22. I was so interested I couldn't lay the book down. 23. Who borrowed my book? 24. I found the book very hard to read. 25. Most men like detective stories.

316. *Magazines

1. My subscription to the magazine has expired. 2. There were no magazines sold on the train. 3. Magazine advertisements are often a work of art. 4. Which magazine has the best serial stories? 5. How much did you pay for The Saturday Evening Post in Paris? 6. You can borrow the magazine from the Library. 7. There isn't time to read all the magazines that come to the house. 8. I buy only the magazines that have articles that interest me. 9. Which magazines would you like for your journey? 10. Success stories become very tiresome after awhile. 11. Some of the best sellers first appear as serials in magazines. 12. Which magazine pays the highest rates for its contributed articles? 13. How much will a full-page advertisement in the magazine cost? 14. Subscriptions to the magazine have doubled this year. 15. The magazines accumulate very rapidly. 16. I always give away the magazines when they have been read. 17. Which humorous magazine shall I buy for you? 18. I wouldn't be seen reading that magazine! 19.

* It is suggested that sentences be given using the names of as many magazines as possible, and that they form a basis of conversation.

All the latest magazines are on the library table. 20. A subscription to a favorite magazine makes a good Christmas present. 21. When will the (name of any magazine) be on sale? 22. The magazine was late this month. 23. I left money for my magazines to be forwarded to me. 24. The story was refused by several magazines before it was finally accepted. 25. I left my magazine on the chair.

317.   Clothes

1. You will want your best clothes for the house party. 2. Will the men ever wear sensible clothes in hot weather? 3. Where can I buy sports clothes? 4. Everyone wore informal dress at the dinner. 5. The slippers were a perfect match for the gown. 6. Wide-brim hats are flattering to many women. 7. Changes in style benefit the manufacturers and merchants. 8. I hope the rain did not spoil your Panama. 9. He wore white flannels on the tennis court. 10. It was too warm even for a top coat. 11. We took only enough clothes for the week. 12. We wore our oldest things at camp. 13. You will need a warm coat for the boat trip. 14. Did you buy that dress in

Paris? 15. The shops are having sales of dresses this week. 16. Cotton clothes are cooler than silk in hot weather. 17. We were glad we had our raincoats with us. 18. The scarf gave a touch of color to the costume. 19. The boys wore a jersey and shorts in camp. 20. We dressed all in white while in the Tropics. 21. The children wore only sun suits on the beach. 22. Shall I bring some gloves to you from Paris? 23. The fur coat should be sent to storage before warm weather. 24. We almost lived in our bathing suits last summer. 25. Do you think long or short dresses should be worn for evening?

318. Telephone

1. It seems to me that the telephone rings all day. 2. We have just had a private phone installed. 3. There is an extension on each floor. 4. I'll give you a ring the first thing in the morning. 5. I had a perfect connection between New York and San Francisco. 6. Operator gave me the wrong number three times. 7. The storm put all the telephones out of commission for several hours. 8. You will find the number in the telephone directory. 9. The

children keep the telephone wires busy after school hours. 10. We had such a poor connection I could not hear you. 11. I telephoned from a sound-proof booth. 12. How did we ever live and carry on business without the telephone? 13. Where can I reach you by telephone? 14. In the country everyone listens in when the telephone rings. 15. We have a two-party line. 16. It took me five minutes to get the operator. 17. I always telephone my telegrams. 18. I could not hear you because of the noise from the street. 19. One can learn to hear over the telephone even in a very noisy place. 20. Your voice did not sound at all natural. 21. The news over the telephone was a great shock to me. 22. Will you please answer the phone? 23. The phone rang just as I came in the door. 24. Both phones were ringing at once. 25. The invitations to the party were given over the telephone.

319.   NEWSPAPERS

1. The morning paper is delivered to the door. 2. Which part of the paper do you read first? 3. The Sports Section gave last minute returns from the football games. 4. Be sure to

buy the final edition of the paper. 5. Whose column do you enjoy most? 6. Do you refuse to read a paper because you disagree with the editorials? 7. I like a paper that gives the foreign news. 8. The Sunday paper has many interesting features. 9. The musical programs for the week are given in the Sunday paper. 10. A trip through a newspaper plant is most interesting. 11. The pictures in the Rotogravure Section were better than usual this week. 12. The tabloids appeal to a large part of the population. 13. Do you believe everything you see in the papers? 14. Radio, airplanes and cables simplify the gathering of news. 15. Newsprint paper made of wood pulp becomes yellow and brittle very soon. 16. The rag paper editions will last indefinitely. 17. My favorite newspaper is delivered by airplane every morning. 18. The Sunday edition of some papers is mailed to all parts of the world. 19. What does the paper say about the political situation? 20. The paper is too sensational for me. 21. A paper from any of the larger cities in the United States can be bought in New York. 22. It is sometimes as hard to avoid publicity in the newspapers as to get it. 23. Please don't forget to bring home the evening paper. 24. The Pullman porter got a copy of the morning paper for me. 25. You may read the paper at the breakfast table if you wish.

320.   Movies

1. Who is your favorite movie actor? 2. Have you seen the latest George Arliss (name any well-known actor or actress) picture? 3. Deafened people enjoy silent pictures more than they do the talkies. 4. We saw the latest news pictures at the Newsreel Theatre. 5. A visit to the studios in Hollywood is interesting. 6. Where was the picture filmed? 7. The talkies have drawn many of the actors on the legitimate stage into the motion pictures. 8. The "beautiful but dumb" actress is not suited to the talkies. 9. Some people go to the movies almost every night. 10. Some of the German plays have wonderful technical features. 11. American-made motion pictures are found in every part of the world. 12. Lawrence Tibbit's voice in The Rogue Song was reproduced perfectly. 13. Will Rogers has a splendid voice for the talkies. 14. The entire picture is in technicolor. 15. We enjoyed the pictures

of animal life in Africa. 16. The Covered Wagon was an epic among motion pictures. 17. Who was the inventor of the motion picture? 18. Often a fortune is spent on the production of a picture. 19. What becomes of the famous child-actors in the movies? 20. Do you go to a movie play at regular theatre prices or wait until it is shown at a smaller theatre? 21. Every small town has its movie theatre. 22. Who is the best known movie actor today? 23. Will the motion pictures ever entirely replace legitimate plays? 24. Motion pictures give foreigners a false idea of life in America. 25. Let's go to the movies tonight.

321. FLOWERS

1. The old-fashioned garden was a riot of color. 2. There were thousands of roses in bloom in June. 3. The pond lilies were unusually large and beautiful. 4. The larkspur formed a background for the other flowers. 5. Our peonies have never been so perfect as they are this year. 6. You may have all the dahlia bulbs you want when I separate them in the fall. 7. The sweet peas bloom better the more they are picked. 8. We found long-stem vio-

lets in the meadow. 9. There is a border of sweet elysium around the flower bed. 10. I have planted the asters in solid colors in the beds. 11. Our chrysanthemums took first prize at the Flower Show. 12. Flowers must have constant care. 13. The hillside was a mass of mountain laurel. 14. There are purple and white Japanese iris beside the pool in the garden. 15. The forsythia makes a bright spot in the garden in the spring. 16. There were thousands of tulips, hyacinths and daffodils in bloom. 17. Do you like straw flowers for the winter? 18. We found pink and white marsh mallows in the field. 19. There are lady's slippers in our woods. 20. The field of wild azalea was a beautiful sight. 21. We found masses of rhododendron everywhere in the woods. 22. The yellow jasmine made the woods fragrant. 23. The fields were white with daisies. 24. We found both pink and white dogwood when we were out driving. 25. Queen Anne's lace grew along the roadside.

322. STOCK MARKET

1. I want to buy some stock. 2. Why don't you buy a bond? 3. I cannot decide whether

to buy a railroad or an industrial bond. 4. I bought ten shares of National Biscuit common. 5. What dividend does it pay? 6. Is the dividend paid quarterly? 7. What is the yield on the bond? 8. Is the interest paid semi-annually? 9. Is the stock listed on the New York or Chicago Exchange? 10. The stock is traded on the New York Curb. 11. Public utilities companies have some strong preferred stocks. 12. Their preferred stock is a good investment. 13. That stock is considered highly speculative. 14. The best practise is to diversify your investments. 15. Railroad bonds are high grade investments. 16. Is the bond registered? 17. Standard Oil of New Jersey, Common, sold off two points today. 18. What was the closing price? 19. What is the rate on United States Steel, Preferred? 20. The broker has called for more margin. 21. Their common stock has no-par value. 22. Bethlehem Steel have offered stock rights to their present stockholders. 23. Our company is offering some short-term, five per cent, gold notes today. 24. I have just bought a Pennsylvania Railroad bond paying $4\frac{1}{2}$ per cent. 25. Who is the transfer agent for that stock?

323.   Baseball

1. Are you going to the baseball game this afternoon? 2. The Chicago Cubs and New York Giants are playing today in Chicago. 3. I saw the White Sox and Yankees play last week in New York. 4. If it rains after the game starts we can get rain checks. 5. If it rains today they will play a double-header tomorrow. 6. You will have to go early if you want to get a seat in the grandstand. 7. I prefer to sit in the bleachers or stand on the side line. 8. I am never at any one place long at a ball game. 9. When I was in college I was always in the rooters' section. 10. We used to yell ourselves hoarse to boost the home team. 11. The umpire has called the game and teams are ready to play. 12. "Play ball! batter up" someone called from the grandstand. 13. "Strike one! Strike two! Strike three! You're out!" 14. The first batter up was struck out in three straight. 15. The second batter knocked a long fly to centre field. 16. The bases are full, with one man out. 17. The runner was put out trying to steal third base. 18. Did you see that man knock a three-bagger? 19. I saw Babe Ruth knock two home

runs in one game last week. 20. There are three men down, and the side is retired. 21. The first batter up for the home team was caught out on a foul. 22. The next batter pounded out a hot grounder to short, and was thrown out at first. 23. I believe the game is nearly over. Do you know what inning it is? 24. I think it is the first half of the ninth. 25. It's all over—will you see the game tomorrow?

PROVERBS

324. The seventy-five familiar proverbs given here may well be studied with profit. Familiarity with the proverbs often makes them easier to understand and more enjoyable. For home practise, let someone give the proverb and follow it, when understood, with a variation of the proverb, or comment. Then the proverbs should be given rapidly, in varying order.

1. A bird in the hand is worth two in the bush.
2. A drowning man grasps at a straw.
3. A fool and his money are soon parted.
4. A friend in need is a friend indeed.
5. A good beginning makes a good ending.
6. A little knowledge is a dangerous thing.
7. A miss is as good as a mile.
8. A new broom sweeps clean.
9. A prophet is not without honor save in his own country.
10. A rolling stone gathers no moss.
11. A stitch in time saves nine.
12. A thing of beauty is a joy forever.

13. All is fair in love and war.
14. All is not gold that glitters.
15. All's well that ends well.
16. All work and no play makes Jack a dull boy.
17. As the twig is bent, the tree is inclined.
18. Better late than never.
19. Birds of a feather flock together.
20. Children should be seen and not heard.
21. Christmas comes but once a year.
22. Coming events cast their shadows before.
23. Don't count your chickens before they are hatched.
24. Enough is as good as a feast.
25. Fine feathers make fine birds.
26. Give him an inch and he'll take an ell.
27. God helps those who help themselves.
28. Half a loaf is better than no bread.
29. Handsome is as handsome does.
30. He laughs best who laughs last.
31. Hitch your wagon to a star.
32. Honesty is the best policy.
33. If at first you don't succeed, try, try again.
34. In fair weather prepare for foul.
35. It is an ill wind that blows nobody good.

PROVERBS

36. It is a long lane that has no turning.
37. Least said, soonest mended.
38. Listeners hear no good of themselves.
39. Love is blind.
40. Love laughs at locksmiths.
41. Make hay while the sun shines.
42. Money makes the mare go.
43. More haste, less speed.
44. Never leave till tomorrow that which you can do today.
45. No cross, no crown.
46. Nothing venture, nothing have.
47. One good turn deserves another.
48. Out of the frying pan into the fire.
49. Paddle your own canoe.
50. People who live in glass houses shouldn't throw stones.
51. Practise makes perfect.
52. Pride goeth before a fall.
53. Procrastination is the thief of time.
54. Sauce for the goose is sauce for the gander.
55. Slow but sure.
56. Spare the rod and spoil the child.
57. Sow the wind and reap the whirlwind.
58. The early bird catches the worm.
59. The eyes serve for ears to the deaf.
60. The last straw broke the camel's back.

61. The proof of the pudding is in the eating.
62. The reward of perserverance is sure.
63. The worm will turn.
64. There's many a slip 'twixt the cup and the lip.
65. Time and tide wait for no man.
66. Time is money.
67. Well begun is half done.
68. What can't be cured must be endured.
69. When poverty comes in at the door love flies out at the window.
70. When the cat is away the mice will play.
71. Where there's a will, there's a way.
72. Where there's smoke, there's fire.
73. While there's life, there's hope.
74. You may lead a horse to water, but you cannot make him drink.
75. Zeal without knowledge is the sister of folly.

ADDITIONAL HOMOPHENOUS WORDS

325. Practise with homophenous words gives the best all around training in lip-reading that can be had. The student should memorize the words in each group of an assignment for a lesson, and then have someone put the words into sentences. He should be shown the first word of the group, so that he may have a clue, and then all of the words should be used in sentences, not taking them in their order. The sentences should not be repeated, and one sentence should follow another as quickly as the thought is understood. The special word around which the sentence is built should not be repeated. If the sentences are given quickly, one after the other, the student will get training in the power of association (he knows one word of the group), in thought-getting, in quickness, alertness and concentration.

Familiarity with the homophenous sounds and the ability to quickly substitute a word when the wrong one has been understood, are tremendous helps in understanding conversation. A helpful form of practise is to cover all but one word of a group and then try to think of all the words that look like it. Detailed instructions for making homophenous words, and a list of the homophenous consonants will be found on pp. 175-179.

326.

(1) Two words in a group:
abuse, amuse
allowed, aloud
bloom, plume
chamois, shabby
council, counsel
crease, grease
dazzle, tassel
draft, draught
falls, false
ferry, very
fogs, fox
grand, grant
guessed, guest
handsome, hansom
home, hope
lessen, lesson

HOMOPHENOUS WORDS

liar, lyre
myth, pith
nerve, turf
omen, open
one, won
phonograph, photograph
profit, prophet
rough, ruff
shame, shape
sin, sit
smoke, spoke
smudge, sponge
suite, sweet
thawed, thought

(2) Three words in a group:
abound, about, amount
act, hacked, hanged
ascend, ascent, assent
beach, beech, peach
bird, burn, pert
blush, plunge, plush
chain, jade, shade
clam, clamp, clap
cold, colt, gold
crack, crag, crank
croup, groom, group

ear, hear, here
elm, helm, help
float, flowed, flown
foul, fowl, vowel
hoes, hose, owes
idle, idol, idyl
jiggle, jingle, shingle
lack, lag, lank
luck, lug, lung
meal, peal, peel
rabbit, rabid, rapid
ran, rant, rat
roam, robe, rope
run, runt, rut
search, serge, surge
shone, showed, shown
slab, slam, slap
sleight, slide, slight
snare, stair, stare
some, sum, sup
thick, thing, think
throat, throne, thrown
tread, dread, trend
wish, which, witch

(3) Four words in a group:
air, hair, hare, heir

HOMOPHENOUS WORDS

all, awl, hall, haul
battle, paddle, mantel, mantle
beak, meek, peak, peek
birch, merge, purge, perch
black, blank, plank, plaque
cab, camp, cap, gap
choose, chews, juice, shoes
come, cub, cup, gum
creed, greed, green, greet
crutch, crunch, crush, grudge
colonel, kernel, curdle, girdle
dale, nail, tail, tale
dame, name, tame, tape
deep, deem, team, teem
die, dye, tie, nigh
ground, crowd, crown, crowned
him, hip, hymn, imp
hinge, hitch, inch, itch
honor, odder, otter, hotter
raise, race, rays, raze
rank, rack, rag, rang
sack, sag, sang, sank
scene, seat, seed, seen
spine, smite, spied, spite
stud, stun, stunt, stunned
straight, strained, strait, strayed
truck, drug, drunk, trunk
wad, wan, wand, what

(4) Five words in a group:
   beer, bier, mere, peer, pier
   braid, brain, brayed, prate, prayed
   bustle, muscle, mussel, muzzle, puzzle
   chewed, chute, June, jute, shoot
   crab, cram, cramp, grab, gramme
   dim, dip, tip, nip, nib
   dose, doze, toes, nose, knows
   guide, guyed, kind, kine, kite
   hues, hews, ewes, yews, use
   missile, missal, mistle, pistil, pistol
   nags, tacks, tanks, tax, tags
   neat, knead, need, dean, deed
   plant, bland, plaid, plan, plant
   rig, rick, ring, rink, wring
   right, ride, rind, rite, write
   staid, stayed, stained, state
   whig, wick, wig, wing, wink
   white, whine, wide, wind, wine

(5) Six words in a group:
   add, at, had, hand, hat, ant
   badge, batch, match, patch, mash, Madge
   bare, bear, mare, pair, pare, pear
   can, canned, cant, can't, cad, cat
   knot, nod, not, dot, tot, don
   raid, rain, rained, rate, reign, reigned

HOMOPHENOUS WORDS

(6) Seven words in a group:
   brick, brig, bring, brink, prick, prig, prink
   bud, but, bun, butt, mud, pun, punt
   dab, dam, damp, nap, nab, tab, tap
   gild, gilt, guilt, killed, kiln, kilt
   pomp, palm, balm, bob, mop, pop, mob
   side, cite, sighed, sight, sign, signed, site
   wed, wen, wend, went, wet, when, whet

(7) Eight words in a group:
   don't, dote, tone, toned, towed, toad, note, known
   medal, meddle, mettle, metal, pedal, peddle, petal, mental

(8) Nine words in a group:
   bead, bean, beat, beet, mean, meat, meet, peat, mien
   baize, base, bass, bays, mace, maize, maze, pace, pays
   dew, due, do, to, too, two, new, knew, knu
   buck, bug, bunk, muck, pug, bung, monk, mug, punk

(9) Ten words in a group:
   boat, bone, bode, mode, moan, mote, moat, mowed, mown, moaned

(10) Twelve words in a group:
   bite, bide, bind, mite, might, mind, mine, mined, pied, pint, pine, pined

(11) Thirteen words in a group:
   bed, bet, bend, bent, met, men, mend, meant, pen, pet, pent, pend, penned

   fade, fane, fate, feint, faint, feign, feigned, fete, fain, vein, vain, veined, vane

(12) Fourteen words in a group:
   bad, bat, ban, band, banned, mat, mad, man, manned, pad, pat, pan, pant, panned

Part III
FOR THE TEACHER

FOR THE TEACHER

General Principles

THE purpose of this section is to give some suggestions to teachers as to methods of using "Lip-Reading Principles and Practise" to best advantage. The individuality of both teacher and pupil make it impossible to give these suggestions as "commandments."

Successfully to teach lip-reading requires on the part of the teacher a two-fold ability, first, to impart knowledge, second, to develop skill. Some fundamental principles of teaching, which apply to all instruction, may well be stated and should be taken closely to heart.

To Impart Knowledge

(1) Show, demonstrate, to the eye whenever possible; do not merely explain.

(2) Show by comparison and contrast.

(3) Illustrate by examples.

(4) Repeat; repeat explanations, demonstrations, illustrations; but let each repetition

either add something new, or else consider the subject from a new standpoint.

To Impart Skill

(5) Make the student actually do the thing that is to be done. Emphasize the practical over the theoretical.

(6) Repeat, repeat, and re-repeat the process until it becomes a habit.

(7) Develop quick reaction, rapidity of thought and action.

As applied to the teaching of lip-reading, these fundamental principles mean (among other things):

(1) Do not merely explain and describe the movements; show the pupil on your own mouth just what the movement is.

(2) Show a movement by comparison or contrast with other movements whenever possible.

(3) Do not merely name a sound, e.g., short ĕ, but illustrate by putting it in a word, as "bet."

(4) Do not be satisfied with one explanation or demonstration of a movement, but repeat in different ways until you are sure the pupil understands.

(5) Spend little time in explaining the theory; spend much time in making the pupil actually read the lips, for words, for sentences, for stories, for exercises.

(6) Repeat words, sentences, stories, exercises many times. Insist on such repetition in mirror practise on the part of the student.

(7) Give nothing very slowly, neither words nor sentences, stories or exercises, and always try to increase the speed as the ability of the pupil may allow. In anything that is to be repeated after you by the pupil, insist upon a quick response.

Study these principles of teaching, affirm them constantly, put them into practise, and grow into their spirit.

Note: The above principles are taken from "Teachers' Handbook to Lessons in Lip-Reading," published by E. B. Nitchie in 1909.

Teaching Aims

The chapter, *The Eye as a Substitute for Deaf Ears,* tells the underlying basis for success in lip-reading. The teacher should know how to develop the requisite qualities in each pupil to the utmost. Everyone has three sides, the physical, the mental, the spiritual. It is a truism that perfect development exists only when the development of each side is symmetrical. It is so in lip-reading. The eyes (physical), the mind, and even the soul qualities, must all have proper attention to attain the highest success possible in each individual case.

The eyes must be trained (1) to be accurate, (2) to be quick, (3) to retain visual impressions, and (4) to do their work subconsciously.

The first of these requisites is so obvious that there is perhaps a tendency to overemphasize it in the neglect of the others. Of course the eyes cannot be too accurate; the danger is in training for accuracy alone regardless of other needs. To secure accuracy in lip-reading, the pupil must know exactly what to look for. The careful description of each movement tells him this; and the teacher should also show it to him on the mouth. The *movement words,* in which each new movement is developed in contrast and in connection with previously studied movements, provide the best possible material for training in accuracy. The *contrast words* also, by showing the differences between similar movements, direct the eyes to an accurate study of the decisive characteristics. And the *practise words,* giving each new movement in combination with all the fundamental movements, both before and after, show how the movements are mutually modified by association. Directions for using this material are given in their proper place.

Accuracy alone is not sufficient. The quickness of natural speech makes it imperative that the eyes be trained to be quick. For this reason, from the very first, all forms of exercise of whatever kind should be practised always as rapidly as the ability of the pupil will allow. Particularly all review work should be rapid. It will be easier for the pupil to have the teacher enunciate slowly, but the rapid enunciation, up to the limit of the pupil's ability, will do him considerably more good.

The importance of training the visual memory is clear from the fact that often the lip-reader will get the first part of a sentence from the last; that is, the understanding of a few words toward the end of a sentence, aided by the memory of preceding facial movements, will enable the lip-reader to construct the whole. Sentence practise is always good for developing this power; but at no time should the pupil be allowed to interrupt the teacher until either a whole sentence, or at least a clause, has been completed. Other practise for developing the power of visual memory will be found directed under the vowel and consonant exercises, where the pupil is required to carry three, four or even five unrelated words in mind and to repeat them in order.

All this work for the eyes is in its essence analytic. The conscious work of the mind in lip-reading, however, must be synthetic. Hence the eyes must be trained to do their work subconsciously. To do so, the eyes must work by habit, and to form these habits much repetition in practise is necessary. To give an exercise once may train for accuracy, but not for subconsious accuracy. It is absolutely essential, therefore, that the pupil and the teacher should go over and over things until they are truly mastered.

The essentials in training the mind are to develop (1) synthetic ability, (2) intuition, (3) quickness, (4) alterness, and (5) concentration.

The necessity of synthetic ability has been sufficiently explained in the chapter, *The Eye as a Substitute for Deaf Ears*. The story work is all intended to develop synthesis, and the question practise is especially helpful. Every kind of sentence practise is an aid.

Closely allied with the synthetic quality is intuition. The lip-reader who has the power of intuitively jumping to the right conclusions has a potent aid to synthesis. Good development practise for the intuitive powers, leading the mind to look for natural sequences of thought, is to be found in the use of stories by telling them in different words, in the use of words as a basis for sentences built around the thought suggested by them, in the use of sentences to develop other sentences associated with them in idea, and in conversation and in more formal talks along some chosen theme.

It is just as important for the mind to be quick as for the eyes. It sometimes happens that the eye will see quickly but the mind will interpret slowly. To develop quickness of mind the teacher should insist upon a quick response in all work where the pupil is required to repeat what has been said.

By alertness I do not mean the same as quickness, but rather an openness of the mind to impressions and a readiness for new turns of thought. It is not uncommon to find a pupil who clings to false impressions, loth to cast them aside, even when told they are wrong. Such a pupil should have his attention directed to his failing and be cautioned to guard against it at all times. The skipping practise directed for the stories, and the skipping practise directed for the words and sentences will help to develop mental alertness.

In my wide experience with the deaf and hard-of-hearing it has seemed that the thing most needed by them is access to the spiritual springs of human life. No other class of people is so shut off from these springs, for they are to be found above all else in the mutual intercourse of soul with soul. By the fact of their deafness, such human companionship is denied in very large measure. The deaf are thrown upon themselves and their own thoughts and resources. As they have expressed it to me again and again, they are "hungry" for a real conversation; they are "lonely," though surrounded by family and friends. It is not surprising that morbidness, hopelessness and the "blues," and lack of courage and self-confidence mark their increasing deafness and consequent increasing isolation.

The difficulties of the teacher with a pupil like that are truly of a spiritual nature. It is a hopeless task to try to make a successful lip-reader of one whose "Oh! I can't" attitude stands in the way of every achievement, unless that spirit of despair be supplanted by the spirit of "I can" and "I will." It is true that increasing skill in lip-reading tends to dispel these morbid conditions of mind, but it is also true that these morbid conditions stand squarely in the way of such increasing skill. The mere study of lip-reading *per se* cannot be relied upon to banish the "blues" and lack of self-confidence and courage. So it becomes of utmost importance for the teacher to work directly upon these spiritual conditions. Not obviously of course, still less by nagging; nor yet by pity, nor even by sympathy of the wrong kind, (though sympathy of the right kind is a powerful agent).

I can lay down rules for the training of the eye in lip-reading and rules, though more elastic ones, for training the mind. But rules for developing these desired spiritual qualities cannot so well be formulated. I think, however, I can make some suggestions which will help guide the teacher along the road.

Of course no two pupils are alike in their spiritual qualities or spiritual needs. They are not all as "blue" as he whose needs I have been picturing. But I suppose there is no one who cannot stand a helping hand along the road to cheer and courage.

It is axiomatic that to impart spiritual qualities you must have them. That is why I regard "personality" as the most valued asset of the teacher. A strong personality felt as an influence toward the best things are fundamental qualities of the great teacher of any subject, and they apply with special force to the teacher of lip-reading.

Sympathy of the right kind is strongly needed; not the kind that turns the pupil's thoughts more than ever on his affliction, for that strengthens his habit of self-pity; but the kind that, while acknowledging the affliction, gives the pupil a metaphorical slap on the back, stirs him to stand by his own efforts and work out his own salvation. Many pupils rely on the teacher to do all the work, make all the effort. To say nothing of their lack of effort, their very attitude is an insuperable bar to achievement. Win over such a pupil to work with you and half the battle is won.

Meet every mood of discouragment with cheer and hope. Don't be sparing of praise for good work well done. Don't be impatient with failure, especially if the effort be true. Hold up the bright side of the picture always. Encourage by example of what others have achieved. These are some of the essentials in the teacher's spiritual attitude toward the pupil.

Be the friend of your pupil, not merely his teacher. Take an interest in the things that interest him, and gain his interest too, in the things that lie close to your own heart. Friendship opens many a door to helpfulness that otherwise would remain closed. Be his friend, but don't forget that you are his teacher, too. Don't let friendship make you "easy with the pupil," nor cause you to let down the bars to indolence and weaken the spur to faithful effort. Expect, and let your whole attitude demand, the pupil's best.

The teacher who works in this spirit with his pupils will have the joy not only of seeing them advance more quickly in the art of lip-reading, but also and especially of seeing them live happier, cheerier, braver, and more useful lives.

Note: "Principles and Methods of Teaching Lip-Reading," reprint of an article by Edward B. Nitchie, published in the Volta Review in July, 1916, gives his principles and methods in more detail. This pamphlet may be secured by sending 20c to the Volta Bureau, Washington, D. C., or The Nitchie School of Lip-Reading, 342 Madison Avenue, New York.

Giving the Lesson

The teacher should keep before her mind the fact that practically all students come to the first lesson in a state of rebellion because the lessons are necessary at all, with a dread of taking up the study of an unknown subject, and with a fear that they will appear stupid. This state of mind is the rule rather than the exception, and the teacher must meet it in a spirit of sympathetic understanding and a willingness to make everything clear, so far as possible. Programs for the lessons often cannot be followed at first. If they are used it may take several lesson-periods to cover the ground outlined for one lesson. Make sure that your student understands each step of the work, no matter how much time and patience this requires. The most important thing of all is to win the confidence and interest and coöperation of the student from the start.

In order to make things clear and to help the student to understand what it is all about he should actually *hear all explanations*. If he cannot hear the raised voice, then insist upon his using some hearing device. If he is too deaf to hear at all, then the explanations should be written for him, regardless of the time consumed. Disappointment and mediocre work, if not actual failure, are sure to follow if the student does not understand the explanations and instructions, for it is impossible for him to work intelligently without that understanding. You, as the teacher, must not forget that your students are not lip-readers, but students of the subject, and therefore should not be expected to lip-read your explanations and instructions.

As to preparation for the first lesson, the student should be told what we mean by lip-reading, and what can and cannot reasonably be expected from its study. The following notes, used by Miss M. Faircloth with her students, may be found helpful. Miss Faircloth has given merely an outline of her procedure, for each lesson varies with the needs of the particular student before her. She says the notes are "according to Nitchie, Bruhn, Brauckmann, Reighard, etc."

1. "Lip-reading is the *art* of understanding a speaker's *thought* by watching the *movements* of the *mouth.*"
    (a) Lip-reading is an *art,* and a very high art.
    (b) The main effort should be towards grasping the *thought* in the speaker's mind. "We should get the habit of going as directly as possible to the point."
    (c) In the production of sound the *movements* (not positions) of the mouth make lip-reading possible.
    (d) A reader should watch the whole face of the speaker, but concentrate upon the mouth.
2. The practicability of the art depends upon friends and associates speaking with sufficient animation to show the movements required.
3. Qualifications to be sought and developed.
    Ability to *feel* the sound sensations of speech.
    Ability to *observe,* meaning "The art of noticing."
    Ability to draw the maximum amount of help from *alertness* and *quickness* of the *mind.*

4. Do not strain the eyes. Familiarity with the feeling of the sound sensations will relieve strain. Strain of any kind indicates wrong procedure.
5. Lip-Reading is more of a mental process than a physical effort—*keep the mind keen* and the *body relaxed.*
6. Lip-reading is founded upon the revelation of the sounds of vowels and consonants (combinations and variations) as they appear upon the mouth of a speaker when spoken in words and sentences. The muscles that produce sound move the vocal organs, and when such movements are revealed upon the mouth, and their significance understood, through "feeling" and "seeing" them, this knowledge takes the place of "hearing" them.

There are *three forms* of language and of thought.
   (a) The auditory form; that is hearing it.
   (b) The motor form; that is feeling it.
   (c) The visible form; that is seeing it.

In speech-reading we depend upon the motor and visible forms. It is necessary to know the feeling of the sound sensations in order to recognize them when they appear upon the mouths of others.

In making speech, the muscles, or muscle groups, contract to move jaw, lips, tongue, cheek, larynx, and to expel the breath. To produce intelligible speech, the contractions must occur in a certain order. They form a pattern, as it were, which varies with the sentence spoken, and corresponding to them is the pattern of the sound sensations.

Repeat the following and note the difference in "pattern."

Good morning.

Good afternoon.

Good evening.

Thank you.

I beg your pardon.

I'm sorry.

Excuse me.

7. Lip-reading is NOT guessing. Dependence should not be placed upon supposition, but upon ability to make the most of the movements that may be seen upon the mouth of a speaker.

8. Lip-reading is not a question of reading a single sound, when pronounced alone, but a group of sounds. The ability to grasp several and finally many familiar movements at once, even though they follow one another rapidly and appear as one united group, becomes a subconscious habit through practise.

Lip-reading consists in seeking to grasp the meaning of what is said as a WHOLE, and such skill is the most valuable accomplishment a reader can have. It is by developing these powers that real success in lip-reading can be attained, and it is by working along these lines that the surest way is found, in the end, to the understanding of every word. Such skill is the reward of careful attention and earnest application at every opportunity.

Facial Expressions and Clues

A lip-reader is not supposed to follow conversation until in some way a clue to the subject is found. Experience helps to show how "wits" can assist in this regard.

Watching and studying facial expression as people talk and listen gives practise in anticipating thoughts. To have some idea of what is coming simplifies a reader's problem, as to know the text of a sermon prepares the mind for the sermon itself.

Where the subject is not in evidence, a reader should not wait to be told the theme of the conversation, before trying to find it, without assistance from the speaker.

Should a reader find it impossible to grasp the trend of a speaker's thought, the speaker should not be allowed to proceed under the impression that the conversation is being understood. As soon as a reader realizes the need of assistance, it should be sought by asking the speaker for the topic.

Do not bluff. A bluffer will end in being a laughing stock, not a skillful reader. Be honest with yourself and your friends. Never claim for lip-reading what it cannot do. Spread a knowledge of the fact, that to carry on intelligently a reader must have a working basis where movements are concerned. It is then up to the reader to make the utmost of what is seen.

Lesson Outlines

Note: Teachers should read over carefully the explanatory material that precedes Stories and Lessons on the Movements; Colloquial Forms, Vowel and Consonant Exercises, and Homophenous Words; and Variations of Fundamental Movements and Unaccented Vowels, Colloquial Sentences, Proverbs, and Additional Homophenous Words, for further details of the method of presenting the lessons, and for instructions for home practise.

I.

A. LESSON FOR THE DAY.

1. *The Story*

a. Before the first lesson a student should read the story over to himself. If his memory helps too much when the story is given to him, he should not read any more stories in advance of the lesson. If the teacher thinks some help of memory is wise, but it is not necessary for each story to be read before a lesson, then *five* or *ten* stories should be read at one time and not looked at again until they are given in the lesson. If the stu-

FOR THE TEACHER 347

dent finds the story work very difficult, he should read each story before the lesson, or even study it with the mirror if that is necessary in order to understand thought-wholes.

b. For a first lesson and for those who read each story:

1. Assistant reads the story through smoothly (adapting the rate of speed to the student), with interruption at the end of each sentence if the student does not understand the *thought*. Help of memory may, and should, make this possible.

2. Assistant reads the story again smoothly, having the student interrupt at the *end of the sentence* if he does not know all of the words. He will not *consciously* see all of the words but should get them through understanding the thought. If he cannot get all of the words after a second or third reading of the sentence, assistant puts the thought into other words, or gives a clue word (mak-

ing sure that it gives a real clue to the thought), or uses some voice, or shows the sentence itself. He should not resort to a word-by-word method.

3. Assistant reads the story more rapidly, the student interrupting at the end of each sentence for the thought.
4. Assistant should tell story in his own words, the student interrupting for the thought.
5. Assistant asks questions based on the story; student replies.
6. Assistant reads story, skipping around, i.e., taking the sentences out of order to break the continuity of thought.

c. For those who read ten stories in advance, or do not read any stories at all before coming to the lesson.
1. Shows title and proper names and any very difficult words or phrases to give a clue to the thought of the story. (Proper names are hard for a lip-reader and usually cannot be told from the context.)

2. Assistant tells story in own words, with interruption for the thought.
3. Assistant reads story, with interruption for thought.
4. Assistant reads story more rapidly with interruption for thought.
5. Assistant asks questions based on story; student answers.
6. Assistant reads the story, skipping around from sentence to sentence, or combines two or more stories.

2. *Lessons on the Movements*

a. Assistant explains characteristics of the new movement and shows student by illustrative word. If a movement represents more than one sound, as Lips-shut for p, b and m, all should be illustrated.

b. *Movement Words:*

(1) Read by assistant, and repeated by student, in groups of two or three as indicated, each group several times in different order.

c. *Contrast Words:*
  (1) Read by assistant, and repeated by student, in groups of two, each group several times over in different order.
d. *Practise Words:*
  (1) Assistant reads a few words, while student watches for the special movement being studied. If the lesson is on a consonant movement, the student tells whether he sees it at the beginning or end of the word, or both. If the lesson is on a vowel movement, the assistant should occasionally substitute another vowel for the one being studied, and the student should indicate when he sees the change.
  (2) The method of mirror practise should be explained and illustrated. The assistant should say the words (choosing particular combinations of movements) over as many times as

there are sounds. The first time the assistant says the word the student should watch for the first sound, the second time for the second, etc., until each sound in the word has been watched for. The student will not know the characteristics of movements that he has not studied, but let him watch and see if he can see any movement for the particular sound. The assistant should be careful not to emphasize or exaggerate the word or movement, but to say the word naturally.

(3) Assistant gives a word, and the student repeats it if he can. When the word has been repeated, the teacher gives a sentence containing the word. The sentence should not be repeated. Where homophenous words are given (and such words are indicated by the small number following them, words of the same appearance being fol-

lowed by the same number), the sentences alone will enable the student to tell which is which.

(4) Assistant reads the words rapidly, skipping around; student repeats rapidly.

e. *Sentences:*

(1) Assistant reads the sentences. As each one is understood, he composes and gives one or two more sentences associated in thought with the original sentence. Student does not repeat.

(2) Assistant reads sentences rapidly, skipping around quickly from one to the other; student responds quickly.

B. REVIEW (The same for all classes of students). All review work should be given rapidly.

1. *The Story*
   a. Told in different words.
   b. Read very rapidly.
   c. Questions based on the story.

2. *Lessons on the Movements*
   a. *Movement Words:*
      (1) Read by assistant, and repeated by student in groups of two or three as indicated, each group several times in different order.

   b. *Contrast Words:*
      (1) Read by assistant, and repeated by student in groups of two, each group several times over in different order.

   c. *Practise Words:*
      (1) Read, and repeated, one word at a time, but skipping around and going rapidly from word to word.

   d. *Sentences:*
      (1) Read, skipping around, and rapidly from sentence to sentence.

II.
- A. LESSON FOR THE DAY.
    1. *Colloquial Forms, Vowel and Consonant Exercises, and Homophenous Words.*
        a. *Colloquial Forms:*
            (1) Assistant should show student the *form* with which each sentence begins and make sure he understands there will be one, two or three sentences for each of the auxiliary verbs. Assistant should read the sentences smoothly and the student should try for the *thought* of the sentence as a whole, and should not repeat sentence, form or verb. The response should be given as quickly as possible so that the assistant can go quickly from one sentence to the next.
        b. *Vowel and Consonant Exercises:*
            (1) *Vowel* exercises should be given three words at a time, first taking the three words of the puck-

ered group, as "coon good cawed," going over them several times in different order. Then the words in the relaxed group, and the extended group should be treated in the same way. When this has been done, the three words in the narrow group (taking the words across), and the medium and the wide should be given in this way. The student should repeat all three words.

(2) *Consonant* exercises should be given three words at a time, as "back fag whack," going over them several times in different order. The student should repeat all three words.

c. *Homophenous Words:*

(1) One method of giving these words is to cover all but one word of the group, to give the student a clue. Then the assistant should give the student one or more sentences for each

word of the group, being careful not to take the words in the order in which they appear. The student should familiarize himself with the groups of *words* assigned for the lesson, but should not read the sentences.

2. *Variations of Fundamental Movements and Unaccented Vowels.*

   a. *Practise Words:*

   (1) These words of more than one syllable have not the same drill value as the monosyllabic words in *Lessons on the Movements*. The assistant should use his judgment about giving them for eye-training. In any event, he should give the words, and when the student repeats a word the assistant should put it into a sentence.

   (2) After all words have been used as above, the assistant should say the words, skipping around, and the student should repeat the words.

FOR THE TEACHER

b. *Sentences:*
  (1) Assistant should give sentences and when the student understands the sentence (it should not be repeated), one or more sentences associated in thought with the original sentence should be given.
  (2) After all sentences have been given in this way, the assistant should read the sentences in the book, not in their order, going quickly from one to the other.

3. *Colloquial Sentences.*
  a. The assistant should give one sentence and as many others associated in thought as seem wise. Also, the sentences may be used as topics for definite conversation between assistant and student.

4. *Proverbs.*
  a. One proverb should be given and when understood the assistant should give a colloquial variation of the proverb, or another proverb if it is very apt.

5. *Additional Homophenous Words.*
   a. To be given as directed on p. 355.

B. REVIEW (All review work should be given rapidly).
   1. *Colloquial Forms, Vowel and Consonant Exercises, and Homophenous Words.*
      a. *Colloquial Forms:*
         (1) The method of review of these forms is the same as that for mirror practise, as explained on pp. 168-169.
      b. *Vowel and Consonant Exercises:*
         (1) Skip around in the words of a group, giving three words at a time, asking the student to repeat all three words.
      c. *Homophenous Words:*
         (1) The method of giving these is the same as for the lesson for the day, except that the assistant gives but one sentence for each word.

FOR THE TEACHER

2. *Variations of Fundamental Movements and Unaccented Vowels.*
   a. *Practise Words:*
      (1) Assistant gives words, skipping around rapidly from one to another, and student repeats.
   b. *Sentences:*
      (1) Assistant gives sentences, skipping around rapidly from one to another. Student gets thought of each sentence, but does not repeat.
3. *Colloquial Sentences.*
   a. Assistant gives these rapidly, skipping around, and student gets the thought.
4. *Proverbs.*
   a. Assistant gives the proverbs that have been used in a previous lesson, skipping around.
5. *Homophenous Words.*
   a. As previously directed on p. 358.

APPENDICES

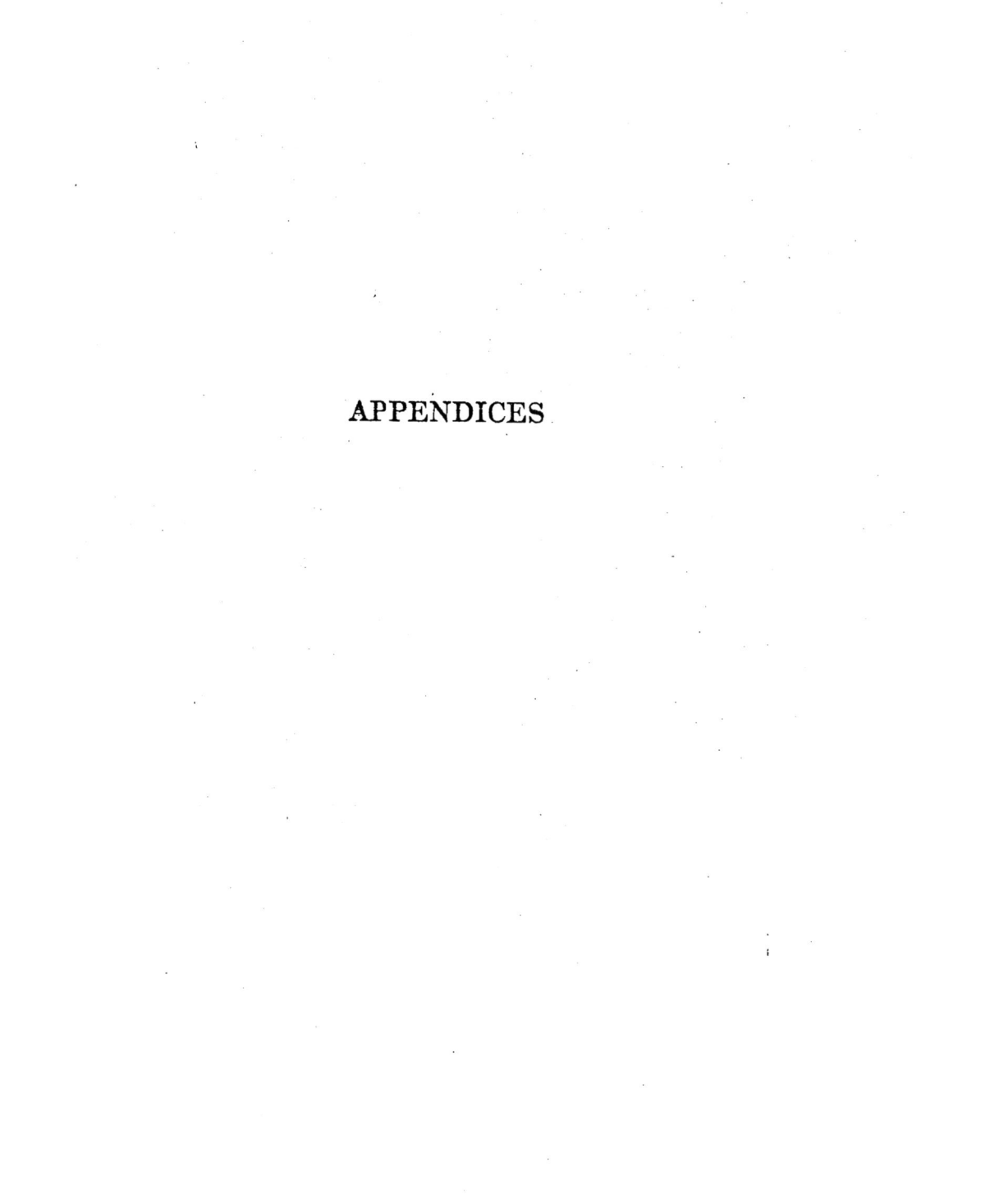

APPENDIX A
TABLE OF VOWELS AND DIPHTHONGS

Accented Vowels	Example	Movements
long ā	face	extended-medium + relaxed-narrow
short ă	mat	extended-wide
Italian ä (ah)	far	relaxed-wide
broad a (aw)	awe	puckered-wide
â before strong r	tare	extended-medium
long ē	be	extended-narrow
short ĕ	get	extended-medium
ē before strong r	fierce	relaxed-narrow
long ī	giant	relaxed-wide + relaxed-narrow
short ĭ	pit	relaxed-narrow
long ō	ope	puckered-wide + puckered-variable
short ŏ	con, off	relaxed-wide, or puckered-wide
ō before strong r	ore	puckered-wide
long oo	too	puckered-narrow
short oo	full	puckered-medium
oo before strong r	sure	puckered-medium
ow, ou	how, out	relaxed-wide + puckered-variable
oy	boy	puckered-wide + relaxed-narrow
long ū	accuse	relaxed-narrow + puckered-narrow
short ŭ	up	relaxed-medium
ū before r	cure	relaxed-narrow + puckered-medium

Unaccented Vowels	Example	Movements
long ā	surf*a*ce	relaxed-narrow, or relaxed-medium
short ă	m*a*terial	relaxed-medium
Italian ä (ah)	sof*a*	relaxed-medium
broad a (aw)	*au*gust (adj.)	puckered-wide, or relaxed-medium
â before strong r	el*e*mentary	relaxed-narrow, or relaxed-medium
long ē	b*e*fall	relaxed-narrow, or relaxed-medium
short ĕ	targ*e*t	relaxed-narrow, or relaxed-medium
ē before strong r	f*e*rocious	relaxed-narrow, or relaxed-medium
long ī	g*i*gantic	relaxed-narrow, or relaxed-medium
short ĭ	pulp*i*t	relaxed-narrow, or relaxed-medium
long ō	*o*pinion	relaxed-medium
short ŏ	c*o*nvince, *o*fficial	relaxed-medium
ō before strong r	*o*ration	relaxed-medium
long oō	t*o*day	puckered-medium, or relaxed-medium
short oŏ	awf*u*l	relaxed-medium
oo before strong r	eras*u*re	relaxed-medium
long ū	acc*u*sation	rel.-nar.+puck.-med., or rel-nar+rel.-med.
short ŭ	*u*pon	relaxed-medium
ū before r	acc*u*rate	relaxed-narrow + relaxed-medium

APPENDIX B

TABLE OF CONSONANTS

The consonants are here arranged alphabetically for convenience of reference.

b, as in "bat," lip-shut
c (soft) as in "cent," extended-narrow
c (hard) as in "cat," throat-movement
ch (soft), as in "church," lips-projected
ch (hard), as in "choir," throat-movement
d, as in "die," flat-tongue-to-gum
f, as in "few," lip-to-teeth
g (soft), as in "gem," lips-projected
g (hard), as in "go," throat-movement
h, as in "he," no movement
j, as in "jam," lips-projected
k, as in "kin," throat-movement
l, as in "leaf," pointed-tongue-to-gum
m, as in "my," lips-shut
n, as in "nigh," flat-tongue-to-gum
ng, as in "rang," throat-movement
nk, as in "rank," throat-movement
p, as in "pie," lips-shut
ph, as in "sylph," lip-to-teeth
q (kw), as in "quart," throat-movement-puckered
r, as in "reef," puckered-corners
s, as in "saw," extended-narrow

sh, as in "ship," lips-projected
t, as in "tie," flat-tongue-to-gum
th, as in "thigh," and "thy," tongue-to-teeth
v, as in "view," lip-to-teeth
w, as in "war," puckered-variable
wh, as in "wharf," puckered-variable
x (ks), as in "box," throat-movement-extended-narrow
x, as in "Xenia," extended-narrow
y, as in "you," relaxed-narrow
z, as in "zone," extended-narrow
z (zh), as in "azure," lips-projected

APPENDIX C

BIBLIOGRAPHY

Instruction Books on Lip-Reading

Bélanger, Adolphe:
La Lecture sur les Lévres; Atelier Typographique de l'Institution Nationalte des Sourds-Muets, Paris.

Bell, Alexander Melville:
Facial Speech-Reading and Articulation Teaching; Volta Bureau, Washington, D. C.

Boudin, Étienne:
La Surdité: Moyen d'y Remédier par la Lecture sur les Lévres; A. Maloine, Paris.

Boultbee, E. F.:
Practical Lip-Reading; L. U. Gill, London.

Bruce and Paxson:
Stepping Stones to Speech-Reading.

Bruhn, Martha E.:
Müller-Walle Method of Lip-Reading.
Manuel de Lectures sur les lévres.
Elementary Lessons in Lip-Reading.

Couplin, Mary:
How to Understand Without Sound.

DREBUSCH, F.:
   Der Absenhunterricht mit Schwerhörigen und Ertaubten; Berlin.
DROUOT, E.:
   La Lecture sur les Lévres; Chez l'Auteur, 19 rue Vayquélin, Paris.
GARFIELD AND MCCAUGHRIN:
   Mentor Practise Course in Speech-Reading for Adults. Adaptable to all Methods of Teaching.
GUTZMANN, HERMANN:
   Facial Speech-Reading; Volta Bureau, Washington, D. C.
HARTMANN, ARTHUR:
   Lehr-und Lernbuch für Schwerhörige zur Erlernung des Absenhens vom Munde; J. F. Bergmann, Wiesbaden.
HEWETT, E. K.:
   Lip-Reading for the Deaf; The Harewood Press, London.
KOOI, DR. H.:
   Het Afzien van de Mond; Gröningen, 1910.
MORGENSTERN, LOUISE:
   Lip-Reading for Class Instruction.
MÜLLER, JULIUS:
   Das Abschen der Schwerhörigen; Johannes Kriebel, Hamburg.
NITCHIE, EDWARD B.:
   Self-Instructor in Lip-Reading
   Lessons in Lip-Reading for Self Instruction
   Lip-Reading Simplified

Lessons in Lip-Reading, Revised Edition, and accompanying Teachers' Handbook; Surdus Publishing Co., New York.

NITCHIE, MRS. EDWARD B.:
Advanced Lessons in Lip-Reading; Frederick A. Stokes Co., New York.

PARSONS, MARY HEPBURN:
The Reading of Speech from the Lips; Akerman Company, Providence, R. I.

RÖTZER, FRANZ XAVER:
Ubungsbuch für Schwerhörige und Ertaubte Das Ableseb vom Munde; R. Oldenbourg, Munchen and Berlin.

STORMONTH, MARY E. B.:
Manual of Lip-Reading; Edinburgh, 1917.

STORY, A. J.:
Speech-Reading for the Deaf, not Dumb; Yellon, Williams & Co., Ltd., London.

STOWELL, SAMUELSON AND LEHMAN:
Lip-Reading for the Deafened Child.

TURNER, BELLE HAMMOND:
Lip-Reading Made Easy.

WHILDIN AND SCALLY:
The Newer Method in Speech-Reading for the Hard-of-Hearing Child.

WOLLERMANN, RUDOLPH, OTTO UND EMIL:
Lehr-und Lernbuch für den Absehunterricht; Teetzmann & Randel, Stettin.

APPENDIX C

PAMPHLETS AND ARTICLES ON LIP-READING

ADAMS, MABEL ELLERY:
Speech-Reading, Proceedings 4th Summer Meeting, 1914.

ANDREWS, HARRIET U.:
Lip-Reading for Adults, Association Review, Vol. 2, No. 2.

BEGLINGER, PAUL:
Absehen, Zurich, 1919.

BÉLANGER, ADOLPH:
Lip-Reading for the Hard-of-Hearing; pamphlet by A. W. Jackson.

BELL, MRS. A. G.:
Lip-Reading; Proceedings, 1904.

BELL, MABEL G.:
Subtle Art of Speech-Reading.

BLISS, SUSAN E.:
Speech-Reading; 4th Proceedings.

DAVIDSON, EMMA F. W.:
Lessons; Annals, 1913-14.

DENNIG, DR. A.:
About Lip-Reading for Deaf Adults; pamphlet translated.

EWING, MRS. GEORGE R.:
Lip-Reading; Teacher of Deaf, February, 1928.

GORDON, AVONDALE N.:
Lip-Reading for Adult Deaf; Reprint.

HARE, MARY:
Lip-Reading; Royal Magazine, January, 1912.

HULL, SUSANNE E.:
Lip-Reading as a Remedy for Deafness—A Review of Gondin's Book; Volta Review, Vol. 14, No. 3.

JONES, MARY DAVIS:
Some Suggestions About Lip-Reading; Volta Review, Vol. 3, No. 55.

JORDAN, SARAH ALLEN:
The Teaching of Speech-Reading to Adults; Proceedings, July, 1914.

KENNEDY, MILDRED:
Mirror Practise as an Aid to Lip-Reading; Volta Review, Vol. 3, No. 55.

KEELER, SARAH WARREN:
A Method of Teaching Speech-Reading to the Adult Deaf; Association Review, Vol. 6, No. 3.

KOBRAK, DR. FRANZ:
Reading Speech from the Face of the Speaker; Sonderabdruck aus der Medizinischen Klinik, Jahrg., 1908, No. 10 (Berlin).

NITCHIE, EDWARD B.:
Principles and Methods of Teaching Lip-Reading, The Physiological Basis of the Visible Movements in Lip-Reading, Grasping the Meaning as a Whole, The Use of Homophenous Words; Volta Bureau, Washington, D. C.

REIGHARD, JACOB:
Speech-Reading—Its Place in Colleges and Universities—its Teachers.

SANDERS, MRS. L. M.:
  My Experience in Public Schools; Proceedings, 1914.
STORY, A. J.:
  The Importance of Consonants in Speech and Speech-Reading; Association Review, Vol. II, No. 5.
VAN PRAAGH, WILLIAM:
  Lip-Reading—What it Ought to Be; Pamphlet Form, London, 1897.
WHITE, HARRY W.:
  The Teaching of Lip-Reading; Quarterly Review of Deaf-Mute Education (British).

BOOKS ON ALLIED SUBJECTS

ARNOLD, THOMAS:
  Education of the Deaf.
BELL, ALEXANDER GRAHAM:
  The Mechanism of Speech; Funk & Wagnalls Co., New York.
  Graphical Studies of Marriages of the Deaf.
  Duration of Life and Conditions Associated with Longevity.
BELL, ALEXANDER MELVILLE:
  Sounds and Their Relations, and also other works on Visible Speech; Volta Bureau, Washington, D. C.

CARRUTHERS, S. W.:
 A contribution to the Mechanism of Articulate Speech; The Edinburgh Medical Journal, Edinburgh.

COLLINGWOOD, H. W.:
 Adventures in Silence.

DE LAND, FRED:
 Dumb No Longer, or the Romance of the Telephone.

FAY, E. A.:
 Marriages of the Deaf in America.

FERRERI, G.:
 The American Institutions for the Education of the Deaf.

GAW, ALBERT C.:
 The Legal Status of the Deaf.

HISTORIES OF AMERICAN SCHOOLS FOR THE DEAF (3 volumes).

LOVE, JAMES KERR, M.D.:
 The Causes and Prevention of Deafness.
 Diseases of the Ear in School Children.

MONTAGUE, MARGARET P.:
 Closed Doors.

PECK, SAMUELSON AND LEHMAN:
 Ears and the Man.

BOOK JUNGLE

Bringing Classics to Life

www.bookjungle.com email: sales@bookjungle.com fax: 630-214-0564 mail: Book Jungle PO Box 2226 Champaign, IL 61825

The Two Babylons
Alexander Hislop

QTY

You may be surprised to learn that many traditions of Roman Catholicism in fact don't come from Christ's teachings but from an ancient Babylonian "Mystery" religion that was centered on Nimrod, his wife Semiramis, and a child Tammuz. This book shows how this ancient religion transformed itself as it incorporated Christ into its teachings....

Religion/History   Pages:358
ISBN: 1-59462-010-5   MSRP $22.95

The Power Of Concentration
Theron Q. Dumont

It is of the utmost value to learn how to concentrate. To make the greatest success of anything you must be able to concentrate your entire thought upon the idea you are working on. The person that is able to concentrate utilizes all constructive thoughts and shuts out all destructive ones...

Self Help/Inspirational   Pages:196
ISBN: 1-59462-141-1   MSRP $14.95

Rightly Dividing The Word
Clarence Larkin

The "Fundamental Doctrines" of the Christian Faith are clearly outlined in numerous books on Theology, but they are not available to the average reader and were mainly written for students. The Author has made it the work of his ministry to preach the "Fundamental Doctrines." To this end he has aimed to express them in the simplest and clearest manner..

Religion   Pages:352
ISBN: 1-59462-334-1   MSRP $23.45

The Law of Psychic Phenomena
Thomson Jay Hudson

"I do not expect this book to stand upon its literary merits; for if it is unsound in principle, felicity of diction cannot save it, and if sound, homeliness of expression cannot destroy it. My primary object in offering it to the public is to assist in bringing Psychology within the domain of the exact sciences. That this has never been accomplished..."

New Age   Pages:420
ISBN: 1-59462-124-1   MSRP $29.95

Beautiful Joe
Marshall Saunders

When Marshall visited the Moore family in 1892, she discovered Joe, a dog they had nursed back to health from his previous abusive home to live a happy life. So moved was she, that she wrote this classic masterpiece which won accolades and was recognized as a heartwarming symbol for humane animal treatment...

Fiction   Pages:256
ISBN: 1-59462-261-2   MSRP $18.45

BOOK JUNGLE

Bringing Classics to Life

www.bookjungle.com email: sales@bookjungle.com fax: 630-214-0564 mail: Book Jungle PO Box 2226 Champaign, IL 61825

QTY

The Go-Getter
Kyne B. Peter

The Go Getter is the story of William Peck. He was a war veteran and amputee who will not be refused what he wants. Peck not only fights to find employment but continually proves himself more than competent at the many difficult test that are throw his way in the course of his early days with the Ricks Lumber Company...

Business/Self Help/Inspirational   Pages: 68

ISBN: *1-59462-186-1*   MSRP *$8.95*

Self Mastery
Emile Coue

Emile Coue came up with novel way to improve the lives of people. He was a pharmacist by trade and often saw ailing people. This lead him to develop autosuggestion, a form of self-hypnosis. At the time his theories weren't popular but over the years evidence is mounting that he was indeed right all along...

New Age/Self Help   Pages: 98

ISBN: *1-59462-189-6*   MSRP *$7.95*

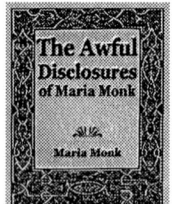

The Awful Disclosures Of Maria Monk

"I cannot banish the scenes and characters of this book from my memory. To me it can never appear like an amusing fable, or lose its interest and importance. The story is one which is continually before me, and must return fresh to my mind with painful emotions as long as I live..."

Religion   Pages: 232

ISBN: *1-59462-160-8*   MSRP *$17.95*

As a Man Thinketh
James Allen

"This little volume (the result of meditation and experience) is not intended as an exhaustive treatise on the much-written-upon subject of the power of thought. It is suggestive rather than explanatory, its object being to stimulate men and women to the discovery and perception of the truth that by virtue of the thoughts which they choose and encourage..."

Inspirational/Self Help   Pages: 80

ISBN: *1-59462-231-0*   MSRP *$9.45*

The Enchanted April
Elizabeth Von Arnim

It began in a woman's club in London on a February afternoon, an uncomfortable club, and a miserable afternoon when Mrs. Wilkins, who had come down from Hampstead to shop and had lunched at her club, took up The Times from the table in the smoking-room...

Fiction   Pages: 368

ISBN: *1-59462-150-0*   MSRP *$23.45*

Bringing Classics to Life

BOOK JUNGLE

www.bookjungle.com email: sales@bookjungle.com fax: 630-214-0564 mail: Book Jungle PO Box 2226 Champaign, IL 61825

The Codes Of Hammurabi And Moses - W. W. Davies

The discovery of the Hammurabi Code is one of the greatest achievements of archaeology, and is of paramount interest, not only to the student of the Bible, but also to all those interested in ancient history...

Religion — Pages: 132
ISBN: *1-59462-338-4*   MSRP *$12.95*

The Thirty-Six Dramatic Situations
Georges Polti

An incredibly useful guide for aspiring authors and playwrights. This volume categorizes every dramatic situation which could occur in a story and describes them in a list of 36 situations. A great aid to help inspire or formalize the creative writing process...

Self Help/Reference — Pages: 204
ISBN: *1-59462-134-9*   MSRP *$15.95*

Holland - The History Of Netherlands
Thomas Colley Grattan

Thomas Grattan was a prestigious writer from Dublin who served as British Consul to the US. Among his works is an authoritative look at the history of Holland. A colorful and interesting look at history....

History/Politics — Pages: 408
ISBN: *1-59462-137-3*   MSRP *$26.95*

A Concise Dictionary of Middle English
A. L. Mayhew
Walter W. Skeat

The present work is intended to meet, in some measure, the requirements of those who wish to make some study of Middle-English, and who find a difficulty in obtaining such assistance as will enable them to find out the meanings and etymologies of the words most essential to their purpose...

Reference/History — Pages: 332
ISBN: *1-59462-119-5*   MSRP *$29.95*

The Witch-Cult in Western Europe
Margaret Murray

QTY

The mass of existing material on this subject is so great that I have not attempted to make a survey of the whole of European "Witchcraft" but have confined myself to an intensive study of the cult in Great Britain. In order, however, to obtain a clearer understanding of the ritual and beliefs I have had recourse to French and Flemish sources...

Occult — Pages: 308
ISBN: *1-59462-126-8*   MSRP *$22.45*

Bringing Classics to Life

BOOK JUNGLE

www.bookjungle.com *email: sales@bookjungle.com fax: 630-214-0564 mail: Book Jungle PO Box 2226 Champaign, IL 61825*

Name	
Email	
Telephone	
Address	
City, State ZIP	

☐ **Credit Card** ☐ **Check / Money Order**

Credit Card Number	
Expiration Date	
Signature	

Please Mail to: Book Jungle
PO Box 2226
Champaign, IL 61825
or Fax to: 630-214-0564

ORDERING INFORMATION

web: *www.bookjungle.com*
email: *sales@bookjungle.com*
fax: *630-214-0564*
mail: *Book Jungle PO Box 2226 Champaign, IL 61825*
or PayPal *to sales@bookjungle.com*

Please contact us for bulk discounts
DIRECT-ORDER TERMS

20% Discount if You Order
Two or More Books
Free Domestic Shipping!

Printed in the United Kingdom
by Lightning Source UK Ltd.
124067UK00001B/126/A